GO IDIOMS AND BEST PRACTICES FOR DEVELOPERS

Go Beyond The Basics:Advanced Idioms and Best Practices For Robust Go Applications

KRISTINE ELLIS

Chapter 1: Understanding Idiomatic Go

1.1 What Makes Go Unique?

Go, also known as Golang, is not just another programming language—it is a carefully designed system language that balances simplicity, performance, and scalability. Unlike many modern languages that focus on extensive features and syntactic sugar, Go was built to solve real-world software engineering challenges while maintaining readability, efficiency, and developer productivity.

A Language Born for Scalability and Simplicity

Go was developed at Google to handle the complexity of large-scale software systems. The primary goal was to address problems such as slow build times, dependency management headaches, and code maintainability in massive codebases. Many existing languages either had excessive complexity (C++, Java) or lacked performance and static typing (Python, JavaScript). Go provides a **middle ground**—a language that is simple yet powerful enough to handle large systems.

Key Features That Set Go Apart

1. Compiled Yet Fast and Efficient

Go is a **compiled language**, meaning it generates machine code that runs natively on the operating system. Unlike interpreted languages such as Python or JavaScript, Go programs execute **with minimal runtime overhead**, offering performance close to C or C++.

However, unlike C and C++, Go has a **fast compilation process** thanks to its simple syntax and efficient dependency management. Large Go projects compile within seconds, which significantly improves developer productivity.

2. Garbage Collection Without the Complexity

Memory management in Go is automatic, thanks to **garbage collection (GC)**. While languages like C and C++ require manual memory allocation and deallocation, leading to potential memory leaks and pointer errors, Go handles this efficiently.

Unlike Java's GC, which can introduce unpredictable pauses, Go's garbage collector is designed for **low-latency and high-performance applications**, making it a good fit for real-time systems.

3. Concurrency First: Goroutines and Channels

Concurrency is one of Go's strongest features. Traditional programming languages rely on **threads** and **processes**, which are heavyweight and challenging to manage. Go introduces **goroutines**, lightweight threads managed by the Go runtime.

- A single OS thread can manage **thousands of goroutines** efficiently.
- Goroutines communicate using **channels**, eliminating the need for complex locking mechanisms.
- The **sync package** and **context package** offer structured concurrency control.

These features make Go an excellent choice for **high-performance, concurrent applications** such as **web servers, distributed systems, and microservices**.

4. A Standard Library That Matters

Go comes with a **rich standard library** that reduces dependency on third-party packages. Some highlights include:

- **net/http** for building web servers without additional frameworks.
- **encoding/json** for working with JSON data seamlessly.
- **sync** for concurrency control.
- **testing** for built-in unit testing support.

Unlike many modern languages that rely on multiple external dependencies, Go's standard library is designed to be **batteries-included**, making development faster and reducing potential security risks.

5. Simplicity in Syntax and Readability

Go avoids unnecessary complexity in its syntax. Features such as:

- **No classes or inheritance**—favoring composition over object-oriented hierarchies.
- **Minimal keywords and syntax rules**, making it easy to read and write.
- **Consistent formatting enforced by gofmt**, ensuring all Go code looks the same.

This simplicity allows teams to **onboard new developers quickly** and maintain large codebases efficiently.

6. First-Class Support for Microservices and Cloud Computing

Go's design aligns well with **modern cloud-native and microservices architectures**. It has:

- Built-in support for **RESTful APIs** and **gRPC**.
- Easy deployment with **Docker and Kubernetes**.
- Cross-compilation to different architectures, making it ideal for cloud and edge computing.

Go is now the foundation of many **high-performance cloud services**, including Kubernetes, Docker, and Prometheus.

1.2 The Philosophy of Idiomatic Go

Writing Go is not just about syntax—it's about following a philosophy that ensures simplicity, clarity, and efficiency. **Idiomatic Go** refers to writing Go code **the way it was intended to be written**, embracing Go's best practices and avoiding unnecessary complexity.

Core Principles of Idiomatic Go

1. Readability Over Cleverness

Go prioritizes **readability and maintainability** over clever or overly optimized code. Unlike languages like Python or Ruby, where developers often use creative one-liners, Go encourages **clear, explicit code that anyone can understand** at a glance.

Example:

✔ **Idiomatic Go:**

```go
CopyEdit
if err != nil {
    return fmt.Errorf("failed to connect: %w", err)
}
```

✗ Non-Idiomatic Go:

```go
CopyEdit
return err == nil ? nil : fmt.Errorf("failed to connect: %w", err)
```

Go discourages **ternary operators** and favors **explicit error handling** to improve code clarity.

2. Simplicity Over Feature Bloat

Go intentionally leaves out many features that are common in other languages, including:

- No **generics** (until Go 1.18, where they were introduced cautiously).
- No **inheritance**—favoring composition instead.
- No **exceptions**—error handling is explicit and predictable.

This minimalistic approach ensures that Go remains **easy to learn, debug, and maintain**.

3. Composition Over Inheritance

Instead of deep class hierarchies, Go uses **struct embedding and interfaces** to achieve **flexibility without complexity**.

Example of idiomatic **struct composition**:

```go
CopyEdit
type Logger struct {
    logLevel string
}

func (l Logger) Log(message string) {
    fmt.Println(l.logLevel + ": " + message)
}

type App struct {
    Logger
```

```
}

func main() {
    app := App{Logger{"INFO"}}
    app.Log("Application started") // INFO: Application started
}
```

By **embedding Logger** in App, we achieve **inheritance-like behavior** without the pitfalls of class-based object-oriented programming.

4. Error Handling as a Core Feature

Go's philosophy treats **errors as values** rather than using exceptions. This forces developers to handle errors explicitly, improving **code reliability**.

Idiomatic error handling:

```go
CopyEdit
file, err := os.Open("config.yaml")
if err != nil {
    log.Fatalf("Failed to open file: %v", err)
}
defer file.Close()
```

By making **error handling explicit**, Go prevents **silent failures** that are common in exception-based languages.

5. The "Don't Over-Engineer" Mentality

Go encourages **simple solutions over unnecessary abstraction**. Unlike Java or C++, where developers often use **factories, builders, and complex design patterns**, Go developers prefer **straightforward solutions**.

5

Example: Instead of using an unnecessary factory pattern, Go allows direct struct initialization:

```go
CopyEdit
type User struct {
    Name string
    Age  int
}

user := User{Name: "Alice", Age: 30}
```

This keeps code **clean, understandable, and easy to debug.**

Go stands out because of its **simplicity, performance, and scalability**. Understanding **idiomatic Go** ensures that developers write code that is easy to maintain, scalable, and consistent with best practices. By embracing **readability, simplicity, explicit error handling, and effective concurrency**, developers can fully harness Go's power while keeping their codebase clean and efficient.

1.3 Writing Readable and Maintainable Go Code

Writing code that is readable and maintainable is an **investment in the future**. Whether you're working on a personal project, contributing to an open-source library, or maintaining a large enterprise codebase, writing **idiomatic Go** makes collaboration easier and reduces technical debt.

While performance and correctness are essential, **clarity and maintainability should never be sacrificed for unnecessary cleverness**.

Principles of Readable and Maintainable Go Code

1. Choose Descriptive and Meaningful Names

Go developers prefer **clear, descriptive variable and function names** rather than cryptic abbreviations.

✔ Good Naming Conventions (Idiomatic Go):

go

CopyEdit

```
type Order struct {
    OrderID    string
    TotalPrice float64
    CreatedAt  time.Time
}
```

✗ Poor Naming Conventions:

go

CopyEdit

```
type O struct {
    id string
    p  float64
    t  time.Time
}
```

Why? The first example is **self-documenting**—you don't need comments to understand it.

💡 **Rule of Thumb:**

- Functions should describe what they do (CalculateTax(), GetUserProfile()).
- Variables should reflect their purpose (configFilePath, maxRetries).
- Use **short, common names** (i, j, err, ctx) **only when the context is obvious**.

2. Keep Functions Focused and Short

Functions should **do one thing and do it well**. A function that spans multiple pages is a **red flag** for maintainability.

✔ **Good (Short and Clear Function):**

go

CopyEdit

```go
func CalculateDiscount(price float64) float64 {

    return price * 0.9

}
```

✘ **Bad (Too Many Responsibilities in One Function):**

go

CopyEdit

```go
func CalculateDiscount(price float64, customerType string, taxRate float64) float64 {

    if customerType == "VIP" {

        price *= 0.85

    } else {
```

```
    price *= 0.9

    }

  return price * taxRate

}
```

Why?

- The bad example mixes **discount calculation and tax application**.
- It **violates the Single Responsibility Principle**—these should be separate functions.

💡 **Break down complex logic into smaller, reusable functions.**

3. Write Self-Documenting Code

Readable code should be **understandable without excessive comments**.

✔ **Good (Self-Explanatory Code):**

go

CopyEdit

```go
func IsUserActive(lastLogin time.Time) bool {

  return time.Since(lastLogin).Hours() < 720

}
```

✗ Bad (Unclear and Requires Comments to Explain):

go

CopyEdit

```go
func CheckUser(t time.Time) bool {
    return time.Since(t).Hours() < 720 // Less than 30 days
}
```

Why?

- The function name should clearly **describe what it does**.
- Avoid using **magic numbers**—instead, define constants like const ActiveUserThreshold = 720.

4. Use Consistent Code Formatting

Go provides gofmt, which automatically **formats code to enforce a consistent style**.

✔ Good (Properly Formatted Code Using gofmt)

go

CopyEdit

```go
func Add(a, b int) int {
    return a + b
}
```

✗ Bad (Inconsistent Formatting Without gofmt)

go

CopyEdit

```go
func Add(a,b int) int{return a+b}
```

💡 **Always run gofmt -w yourfile.go before committing code.**

5. Make Error Handling Explicit

Go treats **errors as values**, meaning they should be **explicitly checked** rather than ignored.

✔ Idiomatic Error Handling:

go

CopyEdit

```go
file, err := os.Open("config.yaml")

if err != nil {

    log.Fatalf("Failed to open config: %v", err)

}

defer file.Close()
```

✗ Bad Practice (Ignoring Errors):

go

CopyEdit

```go
file, _ := os.Open("config.yaml") // Dangerous: error is ignored!
```

11

💡 **Always handle errors, even if it's just logging them.**

1.4 The Role of Simplicity in Go's Design

Why Simplicity Matters

Many languages introduce features that make the language more **powerful but harder to master**. Go takes a **different approach**—it **prioritizes simplicity** to keep codebases clean, readable, and efficient.

How Go Achieves Simplicity

1. Minimalistic Syntax

Go **avoids unnecessary complexity** seen in other languages:

- No while or do-while loops—**only for loops**.
- No exceptions—**errors are handled explicitly**.
- No overloading—**each function has one signature**.

This makes Go **easy to read and learn**, even for beginners.

2. No Implicit Conversions

Go requires **explicit type conversions** to avoid hidden bugs.

✔ **Explicit Type Conversion (Idiomatic Go):**

go

CopyEdit

```
var x int = 10
var y float64 = float64(x) // Explicit conversion
```

✗ Implicit Conversions (Not Allowed in Go):

go

CopyEdit

```
var x int = 10

var y float64 = x // ERROR: cannot assign int to float64
```

📍 This prevents unexpected behavior and makes code predictable.

3. Composition Over Inheritance

Go **avoids deep class hierarchies** and prefers **struct embedding** over object-oriented inheritance.

✔ Idiomatic Struct Composition:

go

CopyEdit

```
type Engine struct {

    Horsepower int

}


type Car struct {

    Engine

    Brand string

}
```

```go
func main() {
    myCar := Car{Engine{150}, "Toyota"}
    fmt.Println(myCar.Horsepower) // 150
}
```

💡 **This keeps code flexible and avoids deep, rigid hierarchies.**

1.5 Common Anti-Patterns in Go

1. Ignoring Errors

Ignoring errors is a **serious anti-pattern** in Go.

✔ **Good:**

go

CopyEdit

```go
file, err := os.Open("config.yaml")
if err != nil {
    log.Fatalf("Error: %v", err)
}
```

✘ **Bad:**

go

CopyEdit

```go
file, _ := os.Open("config.yaml") // Dangerous
```

14

2. Overusing Goroutines Without Synchronization

Goroutines should be **managed properly** to avoid race conditions.

✔ **Using a Mutex:**

go

CopyEdit

```
var counter int

var mu sync.Mutex


for i := 0; i < 1000; i++ {

    go func() {

        mu.Lock()

        counter++

        mu.Unlock()

    }()

}
```

✘ **Unsafe Goroutine Use:**

go

CopyEdit

```
var counter int


for i := 0; i < 1000; i++ {
```

```
go func() { counter++ }()
```

```
}
```

🔦 **Without synchronization, this code may produce unpredictable results.**

3. Bloated Interfaces

Interfaces should be **small and focused**.

✔ **Good:**

go

CopyEdit

```go
type Reader interface {
    Read(p []byte) (n int, err error)
}
```

✗ **Bad (Too Broad):**

go

CopyEdit

```go
type DataManager interface {
    Read()
    Write()
    Delete()
    Update()
```

16

```
}
```

💡 Follow the "one-method-per-interface" rule where possible.

By following these best practices, developers can **write Go code that is simple, readable, and maintainable for years**. Go's **simplicity is its strength**, and writing idiomatic code ensures that teams can **collaborate efficiently without unnecessary complexity**.

Chapter 2: Mastering Go's Type System

2.1. Static Typing vs. Dynamic Typing

When choosing a programming language, one of the most fundamental decisions revolves around its **type system**. Go is a **statically typed language**, meaning variable types are explicitly declared or inferred at compile time, unlike dynamically typed languages where types are determined at runtime. Understanding the differences between **static and dynamic typing** is essential to appreciating Go's approach to type safety, performance, and maintainability.

What is Static Typing?

Static typing means that a variable's type is **determined at compile time** and cannot change throughout the program's execution. Every variable in a statically typed language must have a well-defined type, and any type mismatches result in **compile-time errors** rather than runtime failures.

Key Characteristics of Static Typing:
✔ **Type safety:** The compiler ensures that variables hold the expected types.
✔ **Performance:** Type resolution is done at compile time, leading to optimized machine code.
✔ **Error detection:** Many errors (such as type mismatches) are caught before the program runs.
✔ **Code readability:** Explicit type declarations make it easier to understand how data flows through the program.

What is Dynamic Typing?

Dynamic typing allows variable types to be determined at **runtime** rather than at compile time. This gives developers flexibility but comes at the cost of **reduced performance and increased risk of runtime errors**.

Key Characteristics of Dynamic Typing:
✔ **More flexibility:** Variables can change types, making some coding patterns more convenient.
✔ **Faster prototyping:** Less upfront type declaration makes it easier to write code quickly.

18

✔ **Higher risk of runtime errors:** Mistakes such as passing an integer where a string is expected may not be caught until execution.

✔ **Less predictable performance:** Dynamic type resolution requires additional processing, which can slow execution.

Example: Dynamic Typing in Python

```python
CopyEdit
x = 10     # Initially an integer
x = "hello" # Now a string (No compile-time type checking)
print(x.upper()) # Works fine at runtime
```

In this example, the variable x initially holds an integer but is later reassigned to a string. A dynamically typed language allows this flexibility, but it also introduces risks—if x were mistakenly used in an operation expecting an integer, the program would crash at runtime.

Go's Approach: Static Typing with Flexibility

Go is **statically typed**, meaning variables cannot change their type once declared. However, Go also incorporates **type inference**, reducing the need for verbose type annotations while maintaining the **benefits of static typing**.

✔ **Prevents accidental type mismatches at compile time**
✔ **Ensures high-performance execution by eliminating type-checking overhead at runtime**
✔ **Balances safety with flexibility using type inference**

Example: Static Typing in Go

```go
CopyEdit
package main
import "fmt"

func main() {
    var age int = 30 // Explicitly declared type
    var name string = "Alice"
```

```
fmt.Println("Name:", name, "Age:", age)
}
```

If an attempt is made to assign name = 25, the compiler immediately reports an **error**, preventing unexpected behavior at runtime.

Static vs. Dynamic Typing: A Comparison

Feature	Static Typing (Go, Java, C)	Dynamic Typing (Python, JavaScript)
Type checking	At compile time	At runtime
Performance	Faster execution	Slower due to runtime type checks
Error detection	Early (before execution)	Late (during execution)
Flexibility	Less flexible	More flexible, but riskier
Maintainability	Easier to maintain large codebases	Can become difficult due to unpredictable types

Go embraces **static typing** because it provides **type safety, better performance, and reduced runtime errors**, making it **ideal for building reliable, scalable applications**.

2.2. Go's Type Inference and Best Practices

While Go is statically typed, it provides **type inference** to reduce verbosity without sacrificing safety. This allows the Go compiler to **automatically determine a variable's type** based on its assigned value.

How Go's Type Inference Works

Go's type inference eliminates the need to explicitly declare types when the type can be inferred from the right-hand side of an assignment.

✔ With explicit type declaration:

```
go
CopyEdit
var name string = "Alice"
var age int = 30
```

✔ With type inference (Idiomatic Go):

```go
CopyEdit
name := "Alice"  // Compiler infers type as string
age := 30        // Compiler infers type as int
```

Using := lets Go infer the type without explicitly stating it, making the code **cleaner and more concise**.

Best Practices for Type Inference in Go

1. Prefer := for Local Variables

When declaring local variables inside functions, use := instead of var to keep the code succinct.

✔ Idiomatic Go:

```go
CopyEdit
func main() {
    name := "Alice" // Type inferred as string
    age := 30       // Type inferred as int
    fmt.Println(name, age)
}
```

✘ Non-idiomatic (Unnecessarily verbose):

```go
CopyEdit
func main() {
    var name string = "Alice"
    var age int = 30
    fmt.Println(name, age)
}
```

💡 **Exception:** Use var when defining **package-level variables** or when you need an explicit zero value.

2. Use Explicit Types When Clarity is Needed

While type inference reduces boilerplate, there are cases where explicit typing improves **readability**.

✔ **Explicit typing for API structures:**

```go
CopyEdit
type User struct {
    Name  string
    Email string
    Age   int
}
```

✔ **Explicit typing for constants with expected precision:**

```go
CopyEdit
const Pi float64 = 3.14159
```

💡 **Rule of Thumb:** If a variable's type is **obvious**, use type inference (:=). If the type is **not obvious or critical for precision**, declare it explicitly.

3. Avoid Ambiguity with Type Inference

Sometimes, type inference can introduce ambiguity, especially when dealing with **interfaces**.

✘ **Potential issue with interface inference:**

```go
CopyEdit
var x interface{} = 10 // x holds an int, but as an interface{}
```

✔ Better approach:

go
CopyEdit
var x int = 10 // Explicitly declared as int

💡 If a variable will be used with different types, avoid interface{} unless necessary.

4. Be Mindful of Integer and Floating-Point Inference

Go **defaults integers to** int **and floating-point numbers to** float64, which may cause unintended behavior.

✘ Unintended precision loss:

go
CopyEdit
val := 3.5 // Inferred as float64
var x float32 = val // ERROR: Cannot assign float64 to float32

✔ Explicit typing avoids confusion:

go
CopyEdit
var val float32 = 3.5
var x float32 = val // No issue

💡 Best practice: When precision matters (e.g., for memory-sensitive applications), explicitly declare the appropriate type.

Go's **static typing** provides **safety, performance, and reliability**, while its **type inference** reduces verbosity without compromising clarity. By following best practices—using := for local variables, preferring explicit types where clarity is needed, and avoiding ambiguous type inferences—developers can write clean, maintainable, and idiomatic Go code.

Go's type system strikes a **balance between strict type safety and developer convenience**, making it an **excellent choice for scalable and robust applications**.

2.3. Effective Use of Structs and Methods

Structs in Go serve as the primary way to **define and organize data**, similar to classes in object-oriented languages but with a more lightweight approach. Unlike Java or Python, Go does not support **inheritance** but instead encourages **composition**, which keeps code modular and maintainable.

Defining and Using Structs in Go

A **struct** is a collection of fields grouped together under a single name. Structs allow developers to represent real-world entities in a structured way.

✔ Basic Struct Declaration:

go

CopyEdit

```
type User struct {
    Name  string
    Age   int
    Email string
}
```

✔ Instantiating and Using a Struct:

go

CopyEdit

```
func main() {

    user := User{Name: "Alice", Age: 30, Email: "alice@example.com"}

    fmt.Println(user.Name, user.Age, user.Email)

}
```

🔴 **Best Practice:** Always use meaningful field names that clearly define their purpose.

Pointer vs. Value Receivers in Methods

Methods in Go can be attached to structs using **value receivers** or **pointer receivers**. Choosing the right type of receiver determines how the method interacts with the struct.

✔ Value Receiver (Does Not Modify Struct):

go

CopyEdit

```
func (u User) Display() {

    fmt.Println("User:", u.Name, u.Age)

}
```

✔ Pointer Receiver (Modifies Struct):

go

CopyEdit

```go
func (u *User) UpdateEmail(newEmail string) {
    u.Email = newEmail
}
```

✔ Using Methods in main():

go

CopyEdit

```go
func main() {
    user := User{Name: "Alice", Age: 30, Email: "alice@example.com"}
    user.Display()

    user.UpdateEmail("newalice@example.com")
    fmt.Println("Updated Email:", user.Email)
}
```

💡 **Use a pointer receiver when modifying the struct or avoiding unnecessary copying.**

Struct Initialization Best Practices

Go provides multiple ways to initialize structs:

✔ **Using Named Fields (Recommended for Readability):**

go

CopyEdit

user := User{Name: "Alice", Age: 30}

✔ **Using an Empty Struct (For Temporary Data Storage):**

go

CopyEdit

```
var temp struct {
    ID   int
    Name string
}
temp.ID = 1
temp.Name = "Temporary Data"
```

💡 **Avoid using unnamed struct fields unless necessary, as they reduce code clarity.**

2.4. Embedding vs. Inheritance: Idiomatic Go Approach

Unlike traditional object-oriented programming languages like Java and C++, Go **does not support class-based inheritance**. Instead, Go relies on **struct embedding**, which promotes composition over inheritance.

What is Struct Embedding?

Struct embedding allows one struct to be **nested** inside another, reusing fields and methods **without creating deep inheritance chains**.

✔ Example of Struct Embedding:

go

CopyEdit

```go
type Engine struct {
    Horsepower int
}


type Car struct {
    Engine // Embedded struct
    Brand   string
}
```

✔ Accessing Embedded Fields:

go

CopyEdit

```go
func main() {
```

```
myCar := Car{Engine: Engine{Horsepower: 150}, Brand: "Toyota"}

fmt.Println("Car Brand:", myCar.Brand)

fmt.Println("Horsepower:", myCar.Horsepower) // Directly accessible
```
}

💡 Why Use Embedding?

- **Avoids deep hierarchies** found in inheritance-based designs.
- **Promotes code reusability** without excessive coupling.
- **Encourages flexibility** in struct design.

Comparing Inheritance vs. Composition

Feature	Traditional Inheritance (Java, C++)	Composition via Embedding (Go)
Code Reuse	Achieved via class hierarchies	Achieved by embedding structs
Flexibility	Rigid, deep hierarchies	Flexible and modular
Complexity	Higher, with base classes	Lower, with simple struct relationships
Encapsulation	Often broken with deep inheritance	Maintains encapsulation

💡 **Struct embedding allows Go developers to design modular, maintainable, and efficient code without the problems associated with class-based inheritance.**

2.5. Interfaces in Go: The Implicit Power

Interfaces in Go **define behavior rather than structure**, enabling flexible and decoupled code. Unlike other languages where interfaces must be explicitly implemented, Go's interfaces are **implicit**, meaning a struct satisfies an interface automatically if it implements the required methods.

Defining and Using Interfaces in Go

✔ Defining an Interface:

go

CopyEdit

```
type Shape interface {
    Area() float64
}
```

✔ Implementing the Interface Implicitly:

go

CopyEdit

```
type Circle struct {
    Radius float64
}


// The Circle struct implicitly implements the Shape interface
func (c Circle) Area() float64 {
    return 3.14 * c.Radius * c.Radius
}
```

✔ Using the Interface in a Function:

go

CopyEdit

```go
func PrintArea(s Shape) {
    fmt.Println("Area:", s.Area())
}


func main() {
    c := Circle{Radius: 5}
    PrintArea(c) // Works because Circle implements Shape
}
```

💡 Go's implicit interfaces promote loose coupling and make code more flexible and reusable.

Best Practices for Go Interfaces

✔ Keep Interfaces Small:

go

CopyEdit

```go
type Reader interface {
    Read(p []byte) (n int, err error)
}
```

✗ Avoid Bloated Interfaces:

go

CopyEdit

```
type DataManager interface {
    Read()
    Write()
    Delete()
    Update()
}
```

💡 **Rule of Thumb:** Interfaces should define **one behavior at a time**.

✔ Use Interfaces in Function Signatures, Not Structs:
Instead of embedding interfaces into structs, pass them to functions for greater flexibility.

✔ Use Empty Interface (interface{}) Sparingly:
While interface{} can hold any value, it should be used cautiously to avoid type assertion issues.

2.6. Handling nil and Zero Values Properly

Go provides **zero values** for variables that are not explicitly initialized. Unlike other languages that may assign null or require initialization, Go assigns default values.

Understanding Zero Values in Go

✔ Zero Values for Common Types:

Type	Zero Value
`int`	`0`
`float64`	`0.0`
`bool`	`false`
`string`	`""` (empty string)
`struct`	Fields set to zero values

✔ Example of Zero Values:

go

CopyEdit

```
var num int      // Defaults to 0

var name string  // Defaults to ""

var active bool  // Defaults to false
```

📍 Go's zero values eliminate the need for unnecessary nil checks.

Handling nil in Go

✔ Checking for nil Before Use:

go

CopyEdit

```
var p *int

if p == nil {

    fmt.Println("Pointer is nil")

}
```

✔ Nil Check Before Method Calls:

go

CopyEdit

```go
type User struct {
    Name string
}


func (u *User) GetName() string {
    if u == nil {
        return "Unknown"
    }
    return u.Name
}
```

💡 **Always check for nil before accessing pointers, slices, and maps to avoid runtime panics.**

- **Structs** provide a way to model real-world entities efficiently.
- **Embedding** replaces class-based inheritance, leading to simpler and more flexible code.
- **Interfaces** in Go enable **implicit, decoupled, and reusable code**.
- **Nil and zero values** simplify variable initialization but require cautious handling in pointers and slices.

34

By mastering these **Go idioms**, developers can write robust, scalable, and idiomatic Go code that is both performant and easy to maintain.

Chapter 3: Concurrency the Idiomatic Way

Concurrency is one of Go's standout features, designed to help developers build high-performance applications with ease. Unlike traditional multi-threading approaches that rely on complex locking mechanisms, Go provides a lightweight, scalable concurrency model using **goroutines and channels**. Mastering these concepts allows developers to write efficient, concurrent programs that take full advantage of modern multicore processors.

3.1. Understanding Goroutines and How They Work

A **goroutine** is Go's lightweight thread-like construct that enables concurrent execution. Unlike OS threads, which consume significant memory and scheduling resources, goroutines are **cheap, fast, and managed by the Go runtime**, allowing thousands to run concurrently with minimal overhead.

What is a Goroutine?

A **goroutine** is a function that executes **independently** and **concurrently** with other functions. It is created by prefixing a function call with the go keyword.

✔ Example: Creating a Goroutine

```go
CopyEdit
package main

import (
    "fmt"
    "time"
)

func sayHello() {
    fmt.Println("Hello from goroutine!")
}

func main() {
    go sayHello() // Launches a goroutine
```

36

```
time.Sleep(time.Second) // Allow time for goroutine to execute
}
```

Key Takeaways:

- The go keyword launches sayHello() as a **goroutine**.
- The main() function continues execution without waiting for sayHello() to complete.
- A short delay (time.Sleep) ensures the goroutine has time to execute before the program exits.

Goroutines vs. OS Threads

Feature	Goroutines (Go)	OS Threads (Java, C++)
Memory Usage	~2 KB per goroutine	~1 MB per thread
Creation Cost	Very low	High
Context Switching	Managed by Go runtime	Managed by OS Kernel
Scalability	Can run millions	Limited due to overhead

Go achieves efficient concurrency by using **a small memory footprint per goroutine and a cooperative scheduling model**, whereas traditional threads have higher overhead due to OS-level context switching.

Goroutine Scheduling: How Go Manages Execution

Unlike OS threads, which are scheduled by the operating system, Go uses **cooperative scheduling** with its own runtime scheduler.

- **Go's scheduler multiplexes goroutines onto a small number of OS threads**.
- **Goroutines yield control voluntarily** (e.g., during blocking operations like I/O or time.Sleep).
- **The Go runtime dynamically manages execution across available CPU cores**.

37

✔ Example: Running Multiple Goroutines

go
CopyEdit
```go
package main

import (
    "fmt"
    "time"
)

func printNumbers() {
    for i := 1; i <= 5; i++ {
        fmt.Println(i)
        time.Sleep(time.Millisecond * 500) // Simulate work
    }
}

func main() {
    go printNumbers() // Runs concurrently
    go printNumbers()
    time.Sleep(time.Second * 3) // Wait for goroutines to finish
}
```

💡 **Output order may vary because goroutines execute concurrently.**

When to Use Goroutines

- When performing **I/O-bound** operations (e.g., reading files, network requests).
- When handling **concurrent tasks** (e.g., background processing, worker pools).
- When building **high-performance applications** (e.g., web servers, real-time systems).

💡 **Use goroutines liberally but ensure proper synchronization using channels to avoid race conditions.**

3.2. When and How to Use Channels

Goroutines are powerful, but without **proper communication mechanisms**, concurrent programs can become **unpredictable and error-prone**. Go provides **channels**, a structured way for goroutines to **safely exchange data** and synchronize execution.

What Are Channels?

A **channel** is a typed conduit that allows goroutines to send and receive values **safely**.

✔ **Declaring a Channel:**

```go
CopyEdit
var ch chan int // Channel for transmitting integers
```

✔ **Creating and Using a Channel:**

```go
CopyEdit
package main

import "fmt"

func main() {
    ch := make(chan string) // Create a channel

    go func() {
        ch <- "Hello, Go!" // Send data into channel
    }()

    message := <-ch // Receive data from channel
    fmt.Println(message)
}
```

🔋 **Why Use Channels?**

- Prevents **race conditions** by ensuring controlled data access.
- Allows **goroutines to synchronize execution** efficiently.

39

- Eliminates the need for explicit locking mechanisms (sync.Mutex).

Types of Channels in Go

1 **Unbuffered Channels** (Default)

- Blocks sender until receiver is ready.
- Used for **synchronization** between goroutines.

✔ **Example:**

```go
CopyEdit
ch := make(chan int) // Unbuffered channel
```

2 **Buffered Channels**

- Allows sending values **without immediate receiver** (up to buffer capacity).
- Used when **immediate synchronization is not required**.

✔ **Example:**

```go
CopyEdit
ch := make(chan int, 3) // Buffered channel with capacity 3
```

Blocking Behavior in Channels

- **Sending blocks** until another goroutine reads from the channel.
- **Receiving blocks** until a value is available.

✔ **Example of Blocking Send:**

```go
CopyEdit
package main

import "fmt"
```

40

```go
func main() {
    ch := make(chan string)

    go func() {
        ch <- "Hello" // Blocks until main() receives
    }()

    fmt.Println(<-ch) // Unblocks the sender
}
```

Using Channels to Coordinate Goroutines

Channels can synchronize goroutines **without using sleep or waiting loops**.

✔ **Example: Goroutine Coordination with Channels**

```go
go
CopyEdit
package main

import "fmt"

func worker(done chan bool) {
    fmt.Println("Working...")
    done <- true // Signal completion
}

func main() {
    done := make(chan bool)
    go worker(done)

    <-done // Wait for worker to finish
    fmt.Println("Worker finished execution")
}
```

🔔 **This avoids unnecessary delays and ensures synchronization.**

Buffered vs. Unbuffered Channels: When to Use Each

Feature	Unbuffered Channels	Buffered Channels
Blocking	Sender waits for receiver	Sends without waiting
Synchronization	Ensures immediate communication	Allows delayed processing
Performance	Slower due to blocking	Faster for batch operations
Use Cases	Worker synchronization, request handling	Message queues, task buffering

✔ **Use unbuffered channels when immediate synchronization is needed.**
✔ **Use buffered channels when you want non-blocking message passing.**

Closing a Channel

Closing a channel signals that **no more values will be sent**.

✔ **Example of Closing a Channel:**

```go
go
CopyEdit
package main

import "fmt"

func main() {
    ch := make(chan int, 2)
    ch <- 1
    ch <- 2

    close(ch) // Close channel

    for val := range ch { // Read remaining values
        fmt.Println(val)
    }
}
```

💡 **Once closed, sending data to the channel will cause a panic.**

- **Goroutines** enable lightweight, concurrent execution with minimal overhead.
- **Channels** provide a structured way for goroutines to communicate safely.
- **Unbuffered channels** enforce direct synchronization, while **buffered channels** allow temporary queuing.
- **Properly closing channels** prevents unexpected behavior.

By mastering **goroutines and channels**, developers can write efficient, **highly concurrent Go applications** that scale effortlessly.

3.3. Avoiding Deadlocks and Race Conditions

Concurrency in Go is powerful, but improper synchronization can lead to **deadlocks** and **race conditions**. Understanding these issues and how to avoid them is crucial when working with goroutines and channels.

Deadlocks: When Goroutines Block Each Other Indefinitely

A **deadlock** occurs when two or more goroutines are **waiting on each other** to release a resource, but none can proceed because they are all blocked.

✔ Example of a Deadlock:

go

CopyEdit

```
package main

import "fmt"

func main() {
    ch := make(chan int)
```

```go
go func() {

    ch <- 42 // This send operation blocks forever

}()


<-ch // This receive operation is never reached

}
```

💡 What went wrong?

- The main function **exits before the goroutine has a chance to send data.**
- Since there is no receiver available when the goroutine sends, it **blocks indefinitely**.

✔ Avoiding Deadlocks with Buffered Channels:

go

CopyEdit

```go
package main


import "fmt"


func main() {

    ch := make(chan int, 1) // Buffered channel prevents blocking

    ch <- 42

    fmt.Println(<-ch) // Output: 42

}
```

💡 Buffered channels allow sending without an immediate receiver, reducing the chance of deadlocks.

✔ Avoiding Deadlocks by Closing Channels:

go

CopyEdit

```go
package main

import "fmt"

func main() {
    ch := make(chan int)
    go func() {
        ch <- 42
        close(ch) // Closing the channel prevents blocking
    }()

    for val := range ch { // Receiving from closed channel stops gracefully
        fmt.Println(val)
    }
}
```

Race Conditions: When Goroutines Compete for Shared Resources

A **race condition** occurs when multiple goroutines **access and modify shared data** simultaneously, leading to **unpredictable behavior**.

✔ **Example of a Race Condition:**

go

CopyEdit

```
package main

import (
    "fmt"
    "sync"
)

var counter int

func increment(wg *sync.WaitGroup) {
    defer wg.Done()
    counter++ // Multiple goroutines modify counter simultaneously
}

func main() {
    var wg sync.WaitGroup
```

```go
    for i := 0; i < 10; i++ {

        wg.Add(1)

        go increment(&wg)

    }


    wg.Wait()

    fmt.Println("Final Counter:", counter) // Output may be unpredictable

}
```

🔔 What went wrong?

- Multiple goroutines update counter **without synchronization**.
- The final value of counter is **unpredictable** due to race conditions.

✔ Fixing Race Conditions with sync.Mutex:

go

CopyEdit

```go
package main


import (

    "fmt"

    "sync"

)


var counter int
```

```go
var mu sync.Mutex

func increment(wg *sync.WaitGroup) {
    defer wg.Done()
    mu.Lock()
    counter++ // Protected by mutex
    mu.Unlock()
}

func main() {
    var wg sync.WaitGroup

    for i := 0; i < 10; i++ {
        wg.Add(1)
        go increment(&wg)
    }

    wg.Wait()
    fmt.Println("Final Counter:", counter) // Output is now consistent
}
```

🮐 **Using a sync.Mutex ensures that only one goroutine modifies counter at a time, preventing race conditions.**

48

3.4. Worker Pools and Parallel Processing in Go

Why Use Worker Pools?

Worker pools are useful for **efficiently managing multiple goroutines** while limiting resource consumption. Instead of creating **thousands of goroutines** at once, a **worker pool** reuses a **fixed number of goroutines** to handle tasks concurrently.

Creating a Simple Worker Pool

✔ **Example: Implementing a Worker Pool for Processing Jobs:**

go

CopyEdit

```go
package main

import (
    "fmt"
    "sync"
    "time"
)

const numWorkers = 3

func worker(id int, jobs <-chan int, results chan<- int, wg *sync.WaitGroup) {
    defer wg.Done()
    for job := range jobs {
        fmt.Printf("Worker %d processing job %d\n", id, job)
```

```go
        time.Sleep(time.Second) // Simulating work
        results <- job * 2
    }
}

func main() {
    jobs := make(chan int, 5)
    results := make(chan int, 5)
    var wg sync.WaitGroup

    for w := 1; w <= numWorkers; w++ {
        wg.Add(1)
        go worker(w, jobs, results, &wg)
    }

    for j := 1; j <= 5; j++ {
        jobs <- j
    }
    close(jobs) // Signal workers to stop

    wg.Wait()
    close(results)
```

```go
    for result := range results {

        fmt.Println("Result:", result)

    }

}
```

💡 **Key Takeaways:**

- The **worker pool efficiently distributes jobs** among workers.
- Using **channels** allows safe communication between goroutines.
- sync.WaitGroup ensures all workers finish before proceeding.

3.5. Context Package for Managing Concurrency

Go's context package helps manage goroutines **with deadlines, timeouts, and cancellation signals**, ensuring **graceful termination**.

✔ **Example: Using context.WithTimeout() to Cancel a Goroutine:**

go

CopyEdit

```go
package main

import (

    "context"

    "fmt"

    "time"
```

```
)

func task(ctx context.Context) {
    select {
    case <-time.After(3 * time.Second):
        fmt.Println("Task completed")
    case <-ctx.Done():
        fmt.Println("Task canceled:", ctx.Err())
    }
}

func main() {
    ctx, cancel := context.WithTimeout(context.Background(), 2*time.Second)
    defer cancel() // Cancel after timeout

    go task(ctx)

    time.Sleep(3 * time.Second) // Simulate main process running
}
```

💡 **The context cancels the goroutine automatically after 2 seconds, preventing it from running indefinitely.**

3.6. Comparing Go's Concurrency Model with Other Languages

Feature	Go (Goroutines & Channels)	Java (Threads)	Python (GIL & Async)
Concurrency Type	Lightweight Goroutines	OS Threads	Async I/O (GIL Restriction)
Performance	High (Managed by Go)	Heavy (OS-level)	Limited due to GIL
Memory Usage	Low (2KB per goroutine)	High (OS thread overhead)	Medium
Synchronization	Channels, Mutex, Context	Locks, Executors	Async/Await, Locks
Ease of Use	Simple & Built-in	Complex (Manual Thread Management)	Easier but Limited

✔ Why Go Wins in Concurrency:

- **Goroutines are lightweight and efficient.**
- **Channels enable safe and structured communication.**
- **Context package simplifies cancellation and deadlines.**

- **Deadlocks and race conditions** can be avoided with **mutexes and proper channel usage**.
- **Worker pools** improve efficiency when handling multiple concurrent tasks.
- **The context package** ensures proper goroutine management, preventing runaway execution.
- **Go's concurrency model outperforms traditional thread-based models**, making it a top choice for modern applications.

By leveraging **goroutines, channels, worker pools, and context management**, developers can **write highly scalable and concurrent Go programs** with minimal complexity.

Chapter 4: Go's Memory Management and Performance Optimization

Memory management plays a crucial role in the performance and efficiency of Go applications. Go's memory model provides automatic garbage collection (GC) to manage memory efficiently, while still offering manual optimization techniques for developers to fine-tune performance. Understanding how Go's garbage collector works and following best practices for memory allocation helps in building high-performance applications that scale efficiently.

4.1. Go's Garbage Collector: What You Need to Know

What is Garbage Collection?

Garbage collection (GC) is the **automatic process of reclaiming memory** occupied by objects that are no longer in use. Instead of requiring developers to manually allocate and free memory (as in C or C++), Go's garbage collector manages memory dynamically, improving developer productivity while reducing memory leaks.

How Go's Garbage Collector Works

Go's GC follows a **concurrent, non-stop-the-world, tri-color marking algorithm** to reclaim unused memory efficiently. The key goals of Go's garbage collector are:

- **Low-latency:** Minimize the impact of GC pauses on application performance.
- **Scalability:** Efficiently handle concurrent workloads in multi-core systems.
- **Predictability:** Reduce unpredictable performance drops caused by garbage collection.

Phases of Garbage Collection in Go

Go's garbage collection process operates in three main phases:

☐ Mark Phase (Identifying Live Objects)

- The garbage collector starts by **scanning all active objects** (reachable from variables in use).
- It follows pointers to determine which objects are still referenced.

54

2 **Sweep Phase (Reclaiming Unused Memory)**

- The GC then **frees memory occupied by objects that are no longer referenced**.
- This phase ensures that memory is available for future allocations.

3 **Compaction & Reuse**

- The runtime optimizes memory fragmentation by **reusing freed memory blocks**.
- Memory from deleted objects is **reallocated efficiently** to new allocations.

✔ **Example of Automatic Garbage Collection**

go
CopyEdit
```go
package main

import "fmt"

func createSlice() []int {
    s := make([]int, 1_000_000) // Large allocation
    return s // GC will free memory when slice is no longer referenced
}

func main() {
    slice := createSlice()
    fmt.Println(len(slice)) // Output: 1000000
} // After main exits, GC will clean up slice memory
```

💡 Since slice **is no longer needed after** main() **exits, the garbage collector reclaims the allocated memory automatically.**

Understanding Go's GC Performance Impact

While garbage collection improves memory safety, it can introduce **latency spikes** if not handled properly. The main performance considerations are:

♦ **GC Pause Time:** Although Go's GC is optimized for low-latency, frequent allocations and deallocations can still cause performance overhead.

55

- **Heap Growth:** Excessive memory allocation without proper cleanup can increase heap size and slow down the application.

- **GC Triggering Conditions:** The garbage collector is **automatically triggered** when heap allocations reach a certain threshold. However, developers can **fine-tune GC behavior** using runtime configurations.

✔ **Manually Triggering Garbage Collection (Not Recommended for Regular Use)**

```go
CopyEdit
import "runtime"

runtime.GC() // Explicitly trigger garbage collection
```

💡 **Explicit GC calls are usually unnecessary in Go and should only be used for debugging.**

When GC Becomes a Performance Bottleneck

🗿 **Garbage collection can impact performance in these cases:**

- **Excessive short-lived allocations:** Creating too many temporary objects increases GC pressure.
- **Large heap allocations:** The more memory Go has to manage, the longer GC cycles take.
- **High-frequency GC cycles:** If the GC is running too often, it may be reclaiming memory inefficiently.

✔ **Optimizing GC Performance:**

1. **Reduce unnecessary memory allocations** (e.g., reuse objects instead of constantly creating new ones).
2. **Use pooling techniques** to manage frequently used objects efficiently.
3. **Profile your application** using pprof to identify memory bottlenecks.

4.2. Memory Allocation Best Practices

Although Go provides automatic memory management, following best practices can significantly **reduce memory consumption, improve GC performance, and enhance application efficiency**.

Stack vs. Heap Allocation

Go allocates memory in two main locations:
📌 **Stack:** Fast, automatically allocated and deallocated memory.
📌 **Heap:** Slower, requires garbage collection and incurs GC overhead.

✔ Example of Stack Allocation (Efficient Memory Use)

go
CopyEdit
```go
func stackAllocated() int {
    x := 10 // Stored on the stack
    return x
}
```

🔔 Heap Allocation (More Expensive)

go
CopyEdit
```go
func heapAllocated() *int {
    x := 10
    return &x // Since x's address is returned, it's stored on the heap
}
```

💡 **Prefer stack allocation whenever possible to reduce GC overhead.**

Reusing Memory with Object Pooling

Go provides the sync.Pool package to efficiently **reuse allocated objects**, reducing heap allocations and improving GC performance.

57

✔ Example: Using sync.Pool to Reuse Objects

```go
CopyEdit
package main

import (
    "fmt"
    "sync"
)

var pool = sync.Pool{
    New: func() interface{} { return new([]byte) },
}

func main() {
    obj := pool.Get().(*[]byte) // Get object from pool
    fmt.Println("Reusing object:", obj)

    pool.Put(obj) // Return object to pool for reuse
}
```

💡 Object pooling reduces GC pressure by recycling memory instead of constantly allocating new objects.

Avoiding Excessive Memory Allocation

🔔 Common mistakes that increase memory usage:

- Creating **large slices with default initialization** (make([]int, 1000000)).
- Using **string concatenation in loops**, which creates multiple unnecessary allocations.
- Keeping large **map objects** in memory even after they're no longer needed.

✔ Best Practices for Reducing Allocations:

1 Preallocate Slice Capacity

```go
CopyEdit
numbers := make([]int, 0, 1000) // Avoids resizing overhead
```

2 Use strings.Builder Instead of String Concatenation

```go
CopyEdit
import "strings"

var sb strings.Builder
sb.WriteString("Hello ")
sb.WriteString("World")
fmt.Println(sb.String()) // Efficient string building
```

3 Explicitly Remove Unused Map Entries

```go
CopyEdit
data := make(map[string]int)
data["key"] = 100
delete(data, "key") // Remove to free memory
```

Detecting and Fixing Memory Leaks in Go

Even though Go has automatic memory management, **memory leaks can still occur** if references to unused objects are kept.

✔ Common Causes of Memory Leaks:
🔋 1. Goroutines that never exit

```go
CopyEdit
go func() {
    for {
```

```
    fmt.Println("Leaking goroutine!") // Runs forever
  }
}()
```

✔ **Fix:** Use a **context with cancellation** to terminate goroutines properly.

🔔 2. Unbounded Channel Usage

go
CopyEdit
```
ch := make(chan int) // No buffer limit
for i := 0; i < 1000000; i++ {
   ch <- i // Blocks indefinitely if there's no receiver
}
```

✔ **Fix:** Use buffered channels or close channels properly.

- Go's **garbage collector** is efficient but can cause performance overhead if mismanaged.
- **Stack allocation** is preferred over heap allocation to minimize GC pressure.
- **Using** sync.Pool **helps optimize memory reuse and reduces unnecessary allocations**.
- **Preallocating slices, using** strings.Builder, **and managing map memory properly** reduces excessive memory consumption.
- **Profiling tools like** pprof **should be used to analyze memory usage and detect leaks**.

By following these **best practices**, developers can optimize Go's memory management and ensure high-performance applications with minimal GC impact.

4.3. Using the sync Package for Performance Gains

Concurrency in Go is powerful, but managing shared resources across multiple goroutines efficiently is crucial for performance. The sync package provides **low-level primitives** to help coordinate goroutines while minimizing performance overhead.

Key Synchronization Primitives in sync Package

Feature	Purpose
sync.Mutex	Provides **mutual exclusion** for protecting shared data.
sync.RWMutex	Optimized for **multiple readers, single writer**.
sync.WaitGroup	Synchronizes multiple goroutines and **waits** for their completion.
sync.Once	Ensures that a function runs **only once** in a program.
sync.Cond	Allows goroutines to **wait and signal** efficiently.
sync.Pool	Provides **object pooling** for memory reuse.

Using sync.Mutex for Safe Concurrent Access

A sync.Mutex **(mutual exclusion lock)** ensures that only **one goroutine modifies shared data at a time**, preventing race conditions.

✔ **Example: Using sync.Mutex to Protect a Shared Resource**

go

CopyEdit

package main

import (

    "fmt"

    "sync"

61

```go
)

var counter int
var mu sync.Mutex

func increment(wg *sync.WaitGroup) {
    defer wg.Done()
    mu.Lock()   // Lock before modifying shared resource
    counter++   // Critical section
    mu.Unlock() // Unlock after modification
}

func main() {
    var wg sync.WaitGroup
    for i := 0; i < 10; i++ {
        wg.Add(1)
        go increment(&wg)
    }
    wg.Wait()
    fmt.Println("Final Counter:", counter) // Always correct
}
```

🔌 When to Use sync.Mutex

- When modifying **shared variables** across multiple goroutines.
- When ensuring **atomic updates** to a data structure.

🔔 When NOT to Use sync.Mutex

- Avoid using mutexes for **read-heavy operations**—use sync.RWMutex instead.

Optimizing Read-Heavy Workloads with sync.RWMutex

If multiple goroutines need to read shared data **but only one writes**, use sync.RWMutex to allow **concurrent reads** while ensuring exclusive writes.

✔ Example: Using sync.RWMutex for Efficient Reads/Writes

go

CopyEdit

```
package main

import (
    "fmt"
    "sync"
)

var data = make(map[string]int)
var rw sync.RWMutex

func read(key string) int {
    rw.RLock()
```

63

```go
    defer rw.RUnlock()

    return data[key]

}


func write(key string, value int) {

    rw.Lock()

    defer rw.Unlock()

    data[key] = value

}


func main() {

    write("score", 100)

    fmt.Println("Read Score:", read("score"))

}
```

💡 Use sync.RWMutex when multiple goroutines frequently read shared data but only occasionally write.

Waiting for Goroutines to Complete with sync.WaitGroup

sync.WaitGroup ensures **all goroutines finish execution before proceeding**.

✔ Example: Using sync.WaitGroup to Synchronize Goroutines

go

CopyEdit

package main

```go
import (

    "fmt"

    "sync"

    "time"

)


func worker(id int, wg *sync.WaitGroup) {

    defer wg.Done()

    fmt.Printf("Worker %d started\n", id)

    time.Sleep(time.Second) // Simulating work

    fmt.Printf("Worker %d finished\n", id)

}


func main() {

    var wg sync.WaitGroup

    for i := 1; i <= 3; i++ {

        wg.Add(1)

        go worker(i, &wg)

    }

    wg.Wait() // Wait for all workers to complete

    fmt.Println("All workers completed")

}
```

💡 Use sync.WaitGroup **whenever multiple goroutines need to be synchronized.**

4.4. Profiling Go Applications for Bottlenecks

Performance profiling helps identify **bottlenecks, excessive memory usage, and inefficient CPU consumption** in Go programs.

Using pprof for Profiling

Go's net/http/pprof package provides built-in profiling capabilities.

✔ **Adding pprof to a Go Application**

go

CopyEdit

```
import _ "net/http/pprof"
import "net/http"

func main() {
    go http.ListenAndServe(":6060", nil) // Start profiling server
}
```

💡 **After running the application, open a terminal and use:**

sh

CopyEdit

```
go tool pprof http://localhost:6060/debug/pprof/heap
```

Detecting CPU and Memory Bottlenecks

1 **CPU Profiling:** Identify functions consuming **too much CPU time**.

sh

CopyEdit

```
go test -bench . -cpuprofile cpu.out

go tool pprof cpu.out
```

2 **Memory Profiling:** Analyze heap allocations.

sh

CopyEdit

```
go tool pprof http://localhost:6060/debug/pprof/heap
```

3 **Goroutine Profiling:** Find goroutine leaks and excessive usage.

sh

CopyEdit

```
go tool pprof http://localhost:6060/debug/pprof/goroutine
```

💡 Use **pprof** when optimizing CPU/memory-intensive applications.

4.5. Best Practices for Writing High-Performance Go Code

* **Minimize Heap Allocations:**
  * Use **preallocated slices** to reduce GC overhead.

- Pool objects using sync.Pool.

- **Use Efficient String Manipulation:**
✔ **Preferred:** Use strings.Builder

go

CopyEdit

```
var sb strings.Builder

sb.WriteString("Hello")

sb.WriteString("World")

fmt.Println(sb.String()) // Efficient
```

✘ **Avoid:** Repeated string concatenation

go

CopyEdit

```
s := "Hello"

s += "World" // Inefficient (creates multiple copies)
```

- **Avoid Blocking Operations:**

  - Use **channels** instead of time.Sleep() to wait for events.
  - Optimize **network and database calls** for async execution.

- **Use Parallelism When Necessary:**

  - Use **worker pools** instead of launching thousands of goroutines.
  - Optimize CPU-bound tasks using runtime.GOMAXPROCS(N).

4.6. Benchmarking Techniques with testing and pprof

Writing Benchmarks with testing Package

Go's testing package allows developers to measure function execution time.

✔ Example: Benchmarking a Function

go

CopyEdit

```
package main

import "testing"

func add(a, b int) int {
    return a + b
}

func BenchmarkAdd(b *testing.B) {
    for i := 0; i < b.N; i++ {
        add(1, 2)
    }
}
```

💡 **Run benchmarks with:**

sh

CopyEdit

```
go test -bench .
```

Profiling with pprof and testing

✔ **Run CPU profiling with benchmarks:**

sh

CopyEdit

```
go test -bench . -cpuprofile=cpu.out
go tool pprof cpu.out
```

✔ **Run memory profiling:**

sh

CopyEdit

```
go test -bench . -memprofile=mem.out
go tool pprof mem.out
```

💡 **Use benchmarking with pprof to identify slow functions and optimize them.**

- The `sync` **package** provides tools like Mutex, RWMutex, WaitGroup, and Pool for efficient concurrency.
- **Profiling with** pprof **helps detect CPU/memory bottlenecks.**
- **Benchmarking functions with** testing **improves performance analysis.**
- **Following best practices for memory allocation, concurrency, and string manipulation leads to optimal performance.**

By mastering **profiling, benchmarking, and synchronization**, Go developers can write **highly efficient and scalable applications**.

Chapter 5: Writing Robust and Scalable Go Code

Building robust and scalable applications in Go requires following **well-established software engineering principles**. The **SOLID principles** provide a foundation for designing maintainable and extensible code, while **structuring large Go projects effectively** ensures scalability and long-term success.

5.1. SOLID Principles in Go Development

The **SOLID principles**—originally introduced by Robert C. Martin (Uncle Bob)—help developers write **clean, modular, and maintainable code**. While Go is not a traditional object-oriented language, these principles can be **applied effectively** using interfaces, struct composition, and idiomatic Go design patterns.

S: Single Responsibility Principle (SRP)

💡 **A function, struct, or package should have only one reason to change.**

Each component in a Go application should **focus on a single responsibility**, making it easier to understand and modify without affecting other parts of the system.

✔ **Example: Violating SRP (Too Many Responsibilities in One Struct)**

```go
go
CopyEdit
type Order struct {
    ID      string
    Items   []string
    Total   float64
}

func (o *Order) CalculateTotal() float64 {
    // Logic to calculate total price
    return o.Total
}
```

```go
func (o *Order) SaveToDatabase() {
    // Logic to save order to database
}

func (o *Order) SendInvoice() {
    // Logic to send invoice to customer
}
```

🔔 **What's wrong?**

- Order is responsible for **business logic, data persistence, and communication**, violating SRP.

✔ **Refactored: Applying SRP with Separate Concerns**

go
CopyEdit
```go
type Order struct {
    ID    string
    Items []string
    Total float64
}

type OrderRepository struct{}

func (r *OrderRepository) Save(o Order) {
    // Save to database
}

type InvoiceService struct{}

func (s *InvoiceService) SendInvoice(o Order) {
    // Send invoice
}
```

■ Now, the Order struct only represents data, while different components handle persistence and invoicing separately.

O: Open/Closed Principle (OCP)

💡 **Software entities should be open for extension but closed for modification.**

Instead of modifying existing code to add new functionality, **extend behavior using interfaces or composition**.

✔ **Example: Applying OCP with Interfaces**

```go
CopyEdit
type DiscountStrategy interface {
    Apply(price float64) float64
}

type PercentageDiscount struct {
    Percentage float64
}

func (p PercentageDiscount) Apply(price float64) float64 {
    return price * (1 - p.Percentage/100)
}

type FixedDiscount struct {
    Amount float64
}

func (f FixedDiscount) Apply(price float64) float64 {
    return price - f.Amount
}

// Function that works with any discount strategy
func CalculateDiscount(price float64, strategy DiscountStrategy) float64 {
    return strategy.Apply(price)
}
```

⬛ **New discount types can be added without modifying existing code.**

L: Liskov Substitution Principle (LSP)

🔥 **A derived type must be substitutable for its base type without altering correctness.**

✔ **Example: Applying LSP in Go**

```go
CopyEdit
type Logger interface {
    Log(message string)
}

type ConsoleLogger struct{}

func (c ConsoleLogger) Log(message string) {
    fmt.Println("Console:", message)
}

type FileLogger struct{}

func (f FileLogger) Log(message string) {
    // Save log to file
}
```

⬛ **Since both ConsoleLogger and FileLogger implement Logger, any function accepting Logger can work seamlessly with either.**

I: Interface Segregation Principle (ISP)

🔥 **Clients should not be forced to depend on interfaces they do not use.**

Instead of large, bloated interfaces, **define multiple small, focused interfaces**.

🔔 **Bad Example: Large Interface with Unused Methods**

```go
CopyEdit
type Worker interface {
    Work()
```

```go
    Report()
    Schedule()
}
```

✔ Good Example: Split Interface

go
CopyEdit
```go
type Worker interface {
    Work()
}

type Reporter interface {
    Report()
}
```

■ Now, implementations can pick only the interfaces they need.

D: Dependency Inversion Principle (DIP)

📍 High-level modules should depend on abstractions, not concrete implementations.

✔ Example: Applying DIP with Dependency Injection

go
CopyEdit
```go
type Notifier interface {
    SendNotification(message string)
}

type EmailNotifier struct{}

func (e EmailNotifier) SendNotification(message string) {
    fmt.Println("Email sent:", message)
}
```

```go
// High-level module depends on an abstraction (Notifier), not a concrete
implementation.
type AlertService struct {
    notifier Notifier
}

func (a AlertService) Alert(message string) {
    a.notifier.SendNotification(message)
}

func main() {
    emailNotifier := EmailNotifier{}
    alertService := AlertService{notifier: emailNotifier}
    alertService.Alert("System failure!")
}
```

■ **Now, AlertService can work with any notifier implementation (SMS, Slack, etc.) without modification.**

5.2. How to Structure Large Go Projects Effectively

Why Project Structure Matters

As a Go project grows, **maintainability, scalability, and collaboration** depend on a well-organized structure. Go encourages a **flat, package-oriented approach** rather than deep folder hierarchies.

Common Go Project Structures

1 Standard Go Project Structure (Idiomatic for Most Applications)

bash
CopyEdit
```
project/
|—— cmd/            # Entry points (main applications)
|   ├—— api/
|   ├—— worker/
|—— internal/       # Private application logic
|   ├—— repository/    # Data access layer
```

```
|   ├── services/      # Business logic layer
|   ├── handlers/       # HTTP handlers
|── pkg/            # Shared reusable code
|── config/          # Configuration files
|── migrations/        # Database migrations
|── test/          # Unit and integration tests
|── go.mod           # Go module file
|── go.sum            # Go dependencies checksum
```

💡 **This structure keeps concerns separate and improves modularity.**

Organizing Code by Feature Instead of Layer

For large applications, structuring code by **feature** instead of technical layers improves cohesion.

✔ **Feature-Oriented Structure**

pgsql
CopyEdit
```
project/
|── order/
|    ├── repository.go  # Data access for orders
|    ├── service.go     # Order business logic
|    ├── handler.go     # HTTP handler for orders
|── user/
|    ├── repository.go  # User data access
|    ├── service.go     # User business logic
|    ├── handler.go     # HTTP handler for users
```

■ **This structure keeps related files together, making them easier to find.**

78
```
```

Best Practices for Structuring Large Go Projects

✔ **Keep main.go Thin**

- Business logic **should never reside in** main.go—delegate responsibilities to packages.

✔ **Use internal/ for Private Code**

- The internal/ directory makes packages **inaccessible** to other projects, preventing unintended imports.

✔ **Encapsulate Business Logic in services/**

- Services **act as an API** for business logic, ensuring **clear separation between handlers and data access.**

✔ **Use pkg/ for Reusable Utilities**

- Generic, reusable components like **logging, caching, and validation** should go in pkg/.

✔ **Leverage Go Modules for Dependency Management**

- Always use go mod init to create a go.mod file and track dependencies.
- The **SOLID principles** help write maintainable, testable, and scalable Go applications.
- **Proper project structure** improves modularity and team collaboration.
- Organizing code by **feature rather than technical layer** enhances maintainability.
- **Using internal/, pkg/, and services/ directories** keeps the codebase clean and organized.

By following these **best practices**, Go developers can build **robust, scalable applications** that stand the test of time.

5.3. Writing Maintainable and Reusable Go Code

Maintainable and reusable code ensures that a project remains **scalable, easy to debug, and adaptable to future changes**. Go's philosophy encourages simplicity, readability, and composability, making it easier to follow these principles.

Principles of Maintainable Code in Go

[1]**Simplicity Over Cleverness**

- Write code that is **easy to read and understand**, rather than overly optimized or clever.
  ✔ **Good Example: Readable and Maintainable Code**

go

CopyEdit

```
func CalculateArea(width, height float64) float64 {

    return width * height

}
```

✘ **Bad Example: Over-Optimized and Hard to Read**

go

CopyEdit

```
func Ca(w, h float64) float64 { return w * h } // Avoid cryptic names
```

2 Use Small, Well-Defined Functions

- Each function should do **one thing well**.
  - ✔ **Good Example: Short, Single-Responsibility Functions**

go

CopyEdit

```
func GetUser(id int) User {

    // Fetch user from database

}


func SendEmail(email string) {

    // Send email notification

}
```

✘ Bad Example: Mixing Responsibilities

go

CopyEdit

```
func ProcessUser(id int) {

    // Fetch user

    // Send email

    // Log event

} // Too many responsibilities in one function
```

3 Avoid Global State

- Global variables create **hidden dependencies** and make debugging difficult.
  ✔ **Use Dependency Injection Instead of Global Variables**

go

CopyEdit

```go
type Config struct {
    DatabaseURL string
}


func NewService(config Config) {
    // Use config.DatabaseURL
}
```

4 Use Interfaces for Reusability

- Interfaces define behavior **without coupling to concrete implementations**.
  ✔ **Example: Using Interfaces for Decoupling**

go

CopyEdit

```go
type Logger interface {
    Log(message string)
}


type ConsoleLogger struct{}
```

82

```go
func (c ConsoleLogger) Log(message string) {

    fmt.Println("Log:", message)

}


func ProcessTask(logger Logger) {

    logger.Log("Processing started")

}
```

■ Now, ProcessTask() can work with any logger, making the code reusable.

5.4. Package and Module Management Best Practices

Understanding Go Modules

Go modules **handle dependencies** efficiently, replacing GOPATH and vendoring.

✔ **Initializing a Go Module:**

sh

CopyEdit

```sh
go mod init github.com/example/project
```


✔ **Adding Dependencies:**

sh

CopyEdit

```sh
go get github.com/gin-gonic/gin
```

✔ Updating Dependencies:

sh

CopyEdit

```
go get -u all
```

Best Practices for Package Organization

1. **Use Meaningful Package Names**
   ✔ Good Package Naming

go

CopyEdit

```
import "project/service"

import "project/repository"
```

✗ Avoid Redundant Names

go

CopyEdit

```
import "project/service/service"
```

2. **Encapsulate Internal Logic**

- Place private logic inside internal/ to **prevent external imports**.

✔ Example of Encapsulation

pgsql

CopyEdit

```
project/
|── internal/
|    ├── database/  # Private database logic
|    ├── cache/     # Private cache implementation
|── pkg/            # Public reusable code
```

3 **Keep main.go Thin**

- Move logic into packages and keep main.go limited to wiring dependencies.

✔ Example of a Thin main.go

go

CopyEdit

```go
package main

import "project/service"

func main() {
    service.Start()
}
```

5.5. Designing for Extensibility Without Over-Engineering

The Balance Between Simplicity and Extensibility

- Over-engineering leads to **complexity and maintenance headaches**.
- Extensible design should allow **easy modifications without breaking existing code**.

Avoid Over-Engineering with Minimalist Design

🪦 **Bad Example: Over-Engineering a Simple Task**

go

CopyEdit

```
type ProcessorFactory struct {
    strategy ProcessingStrategy
}


type ProcessingStrategy interface {
    Process(data string)
}
```

- A simple function suffices instead of **unnecessary abstractions**.

✔ **Good Example: Simpler and More Maintainable Code**

go

CopyEdit

```
func ProcessData(data string) {
    fmt.Println("Processing:", data)
}
```

Use Composition Over Inheritance

Go favors **struct embedding** rather than deep class hierarchies.

✔ Using Composition Instead of Over-Engineering

go

CopyEdit

```go
type Engine struct {
    Horsepower int
}


type Car struct {
    Engine
    Model string
}
```

■ Simple, flexible, and avoids unnecessary abstraction.

Interfaces Should Be Minimal and Purposeful

- Define **small, focused interfaces** rather than bloated ones.

✔ Good Example: Small Interfaces

go

CopyEdit

```go
type Reader interface {
```

```go
    Read(p []byte) (n int, err error)
}
```

✗ Bad Example: Large, Over-Complicated Interfaces

go

CopyEdit

```go
type DataManager interface {
    Read()
    Write()
    Delete()
    Update()
}
```

■ **Smaller interfaces improve reusability.**

5.6. Using Generics Wisely in Go

Generics were introduced in **Go 1.18** to enable **type safety and code reuse** without sacrificing performance.

When to Use Generics

✔ **Generics Are Useful When:**

- Writing reusable **data structures** (e.g., stacks, queues).
- Implementing **type-safe algorithms** (e.g., sorting).
- Avoiding code duplication **for similar operations on different types**.

🔋 Avoid Generics When:

- The function **only operates on a single, well-defined type**.
- Code readability **declines due to unnecessary complexity**.

Basic Syntax of Generics

✔ Using Generics in Functions

go

CopyEdit

```go
func Print[T any](value T) {

    fmt.Println(value)

}


func main() {

    Print(42)      // Works with int

    Print("Hello")   // Works with string

}
```

✔ Using Generics in Structs

go

CopyEdit

```go
type Box[T any] struct {

    Value T

}
```

```go
func main() {

    intBox := Box[int]{Value: 100}

    stringBox := Box[string]{Value: "Go"}

    fmt.Println(intBox.Value, stringBox.Value)

}
```

✔ Using Generics in Slices and Maps

go

CopyEdit

```go
func Sum[T int | float64](values []T) T {

    var sum T

    for _, v := range values {

        sum += v

    }

    return sum

}


func main() {

    fmt.Println(Sum([]int{1, 2, 3}))

    fmt.Println(Sum([]float64{1.5, 2.5, 3.5}))

}
```

Best Practices for Generics in Go

1 **Use Generics Where It Adds Value**

- ■ **Good:** Generic **data structures** (stacks, queues).
- ⊘ **Avoid:** Simple operations that do not require type generalization.

2 **Avoid Overcomplicating with Generics**

- If the logic is **simpler with standard types, don't use generics**.

3 **Prefer Type Constraints for Flexibility**

- Constraints define **which types a generic function can accept**.

✔ **Example: Using Type Constraints**

go

CopyEdit

```go
type Number interface {
    int | float64
}


func Add[T Number](a, b T) T {
    return a + b
}
```

- **Maintainability** improves with **small, well-defined functions and avoiding global state**.
- **Go modules and package best practices** keep codebases clean and manageable.

91

- **Designing for extensibility** means **balancing flexibility without unnecessary abstraction**.
- **Generics in Go should be used wisely** to avoid **overcomplicating code** while maximizing reusability.

Chapter 6: Best Practices for Error Handling in Go

Error handling is a critical part of software development. In Go, errors are **explicit values** rather than exceptions, making error handling predictable, readable, and easy to reason about. This chapter covers Go's **error handling philosophy** and best practices for using the errors and fmt packages to create clear and maintainable error messages.

6.1. Error Handling Philosophy in Go

Unlike many languages that use **exceptions** (such as Java, Python, or C++), Go treats errors as **first-class values**. This approach enforces explicit error checking, reducing **hidden control flow** and **improving reliability**.

Why Go Avoids Exceptions

Many languages use **exceptions** to signal errors, but exceptions introduce **several issues**:
1. **Hidden Control Flow:** Exceptions **break execution flow**, making debugging difficult.
2. **Unhandled Exceptions Crash Programs:** If an exception isn't caught, the program **panics**.
3. **Mixing Error Handling and Business Logic:** Exception handling often forces **try-catch blocks**, increasing complexity.

✔ Example: Exception Handling in Python

python
CopyEdit
```python
def divide(a, b):
    try:
        return a / b
    except ZeroDivisionError:
        print("Cannot divide by zero!")
```

🔔 Problems:

- The try-catch block makes the control flow **less explicit**.
- The caller **doesn't know an error occurred unless an exception is caught**.

How Go's Error Handling Is Different

Instead of exceptions, Go **returns errors as values,** making error handling **explicit** and **predictable**.

✔ Example: Error Handling in Go

```go
CopyEdit
package main

import (
    "errors"
    "fmt"
)

// Function that returns an error
func divide(a, b float64) (float64, error) {
    if b == 0 {
        return 0, errors.New("cannot divide by zero")
    }
    return a / b, nil
}

func main() {
    result, err := divide(10, 0)
    if err != nil {
        fmt.Println("Error:", err)
        return
    }
    fmt.Println("Result:", result)
}
```

■ **Advantages of Go's Error Handling Approach:**

- **Errors are explicitly handled** (no hidden control flow).
- **No program crashes** due to uncaught exceptions.
- **Better debugging and logging** since errors are treated as values.

Error Handling Strategies in Go

There are **three common strategies** for handling errors in Go:

1 **Return Errors to the Caller (Most Common Approach)**
✔ **Example: Returning Errors to the Caller**

go
CopyEdit
```go
func readFile(filename string) (string, error) {
    content, err := os.ReadFile(filename)
    if err != nil {
        return "", err // Pass the error up the call chain
    }
    return string(content), nil
}
```

🔔 **Bad Example: Swallowing Errors (Avoid This!)**

go
CopyEdit
```go
func readFile(filename string) string {
    content, _ := os.ReadFile(filename) // Ignores errors
    return string(content)
}
```

✘ **This can lead to unexpected behavior and make debugging harder.**

2 **Wrap Errors with Additional Context (Using** fmt.Errorf**)**
✔ **Example: Adding Context to Errors**

go
CopyEdit
```go
func connectDB() error {
    return fmt.Errorf("database connection failed: %w", errors.New("timeout"))
}
```

💡 Use fmt.Errorf() **with** %w **to retain the original error's stack trace.**

3 **Gracefully Recovering from Panics (Only When Necessary)**

- **Go uses** panic **and** recover **sparingly** (not for normal error handling).
  ✔ **Example: Using** recover() **to Handle Unexpected Panics**

go
CopyEdit
```go
func safeDivide(a, b float64) (result float64) {
    defer func() {
        if r := recover(); r != nil {
            fmt.Println("Recovered from panic:", r)
        }
    }()
    return a / b
}
```

🪨 **Panic should only be used for unrecoverable errors** (e.g., corrupt memory, logic errors).

6.2. The errors and fmt Packages: Best Usage

Go's standard library provides **two main packages for handling errors**:

- errors **package**: Creates and manipulates error values.

- **fmt package**: Formats errors with additional context.

Creating Basic Errors with the errors Package

The errors package provides errors.New() to create **simple error messages**.

✔ Example: Creating a Basic Error

```go
CopyEdit
import "errors"

var ErrNotFound = errors.New("resource not found")

func fetchResource(id int) error {
    return ErrNotFound
}

func main() {
    err := fetchResource(42)
    if err != nil {
        fmt.Println("Error:", err) // Output: Error: resource not found
    }
}
```

📍 **Define error variables (ErrXyz) to improve error consistency across the codebase.**

Wrapping Errors with fmt.Errorf()

For **adding more details** to an error, use fmt.Errorf().

✔ Example: Wrapping Errors with Context

```go
CopyEdit
import (
    "errors"
    "fmt"
)
```

97

```go
func openFile(filename string) error {
    return fmt.Errorf("failed to open file %s: %w", filename, errors.New("permission
denied"))
}

func main() {
    err := openFile("config.yaml")
    if err != nil {
        fmt.Println("Error:", err) // Output: Error: failed to open file config.yaml:
permission denied
    }
}
```

■ **Why Use** `fmt.Errorf("%w", err)`?

- **Keeps the original error traceable** (`%w` allows unwrapping errors later).
- **Adds useful debugging context** (e.g., which file caused the error).

Checking and Unwrapping Errors

Go provides `errors.Is()` and `errors.As()` to inspect wrapped errors.

✔ **Example: Checking for Specific Errors**

```go
go
CopyEdit
import (
    "errors"
    "fmt"
)

var ErrPermissionDenied = errors.New("permission denied")

func openFile(filename string) error {
    return fmt.Errorf("failed to open file %s: %w", filename, ErrPermissionDenied)
}
```

```go
func main() {
   err := openFile("config.yaml")

   if errors.Is(err, ErrPermissionDenied) {
      fmt.Println("Access denied!")
   } else {
      fmt.Println("Other error:", err)
   }
}
```

■ Use errors.Is() to compare errors in a structured way.

✔ Example: Unwrapping Errors

go
CopyEdit
```go
func main() {
   err := openFile("config.yaml")

   var targetErr error
   if errors.As(err, &targetErr) {
      fmt.Println("Unwrapped error:", targetErr)
   }
}
```

🔔 Use errors.As() when checking for specific error types (e.g., custom errors).

Key Takeaways

■ Go's error handling philosophy favors explicit, predictable error handling.
■ Errors are returned as values, not exceptions, making flow control clearer.
■ Use errors.New() for basic errors and fmt.Errorf() to add context.
■ Use errors.Is() for structured error comparisons.
■ Avoid panic/recover unless handling truly unrecoverable failures.

6.3. When to Use Custom Error Types

Why Use Custom Error Types?

While Go's built-in errors.New() and fmt.Errorf() are useful for simple errors, **custom error types** provide:
✔ **More detailed error information** (e.g., error codes, structured metadata).
✔ **Better debugging and categorization** (e.g., differentiating between validation and database errors).
✔ **Error handling flexibility** using errors.As() and errors.Is().

Defining Custom Error Types

A custom error type in Go **implements the error interface**, which requires a Error() string method.

✔ **Example: Defining and Using a Custom Error Type**

go

CopyEdit

```
package main

import (
    "fmt"
)

// Custom error type
type ValidationError struct {
    Field   string
    Message string
}
```

100

```go
// Implement the error interface

func (e ValidationError) Error() string {

    return fmt.Sprintf("validation failed: %s - %s", e.Field, e.Message)

}


func validateUserInput(username string) error {

    if username == "" {

        return ValidationError{"Username", "cannot be empty"}

    }

    return nil

}


func main() {

    err := validateUserInput("")

    if err != nil {

        fmt.Println("Error:", err)

    }

}
```

■ Why Use Custom Errors?

- Adds **contextual details** like Field and Message.
- Helps in **structured error handling** (e.g., API responses).

101

Using errors.As() to Extract Custom Error Information

errors.As() is useful when working with **wrapped custom errors**.

✔ Example: Extracting Custom Error Fields

go

CopyEdit

```
package main

import (
    "errors"
    "fmt"
)

// Custom error with additional fields
type DatabaseError struct {
    Query string
    Err   error
}

func (e DatabaseError) Error() string {
    return fmt.Sprintf("database error: query [%s] failed: %v", e.Query, e.Err)
}
```

```go
func fetchUser(id int) error {

    return DatabaseError{"SELECT * FROM users WHERE id = ?",
errors.New("connection timeout")}

}


func main() {

    err := fetchUser(42)


    var dbErr DatabaseError

    if errors.As(err, &dbErr) {

        fmt.Println("Database Error:", dbErr.Query) // Extract query from error

    }

}
```

■ **Custom errors improve debugging and structured logging.**

6.4. Propagating Errors the Right Way

What is Error Propagation?

Error propagation means **passing errors up the call stack** so they can be handled appropriately.

🔔 Bad Example: Silently Ignoring Errors (Avoid This!)

go

CopyEdit

```go
func process() {
    err := doSomething()
    if err != nil {
        return // Error is ignored!
    }
}
```

✗ Why This Is Bad?

- Errors go unnoticed.
- Debugging becomes difficult.

✔ Good Example: Propagating Errors Up the Stack

go

CopyEdit

```go
func process() error {
    err := doSomething()
    if err != nil {
        return fmt.Errorf("process failed: %w", err) // Wrap and propagate error
    }
    return nil
}
```

■ **Error wrapping helps maintain context across function calls.**

Adding Context When Propagating Errors

Use **fmt.Errorf()** **with** %w to keep the **original error traceable.**

✔ **Example: Wrapping Errors While Propagating**

go

CopyEdit

```go
func readConfig() error {

    return fmt.Errorf("failed to load config: %w", errors.New("file not found"))

}


func main() {

    err := readConfig()

    if err != nil {

        fmt.Println("Error:", err) // Output: failed to load config: file not found

    }

}
```

💡 **Using** %w **retains the original error message, allowing further inspection.**

6.5. Implementing Retries and Fallbacks

Some errors, such as **network failures or database timeouts**, can be **temporary** and should be retried instead of failing immediately.

Implementing Retries in Go

✔ Example: Retrying a Function on Failure

go

CopyEdit

```go
package main

import (
    "errors"
    "fmt"
    "time"
)

// Simulated function that fails sometimes
func fetchData() error {
    return errors.New("network timeout")
}

func retryOperation(operation func() error, retries int, delay time.Duration) error {
    for i := 0; i < retries; i++ {
        err := operation()
```

```go
        if err == nil {

            return nil

        }

        fmt.Printf("Retry %d/%d failed: %v\n", i+1, retries, err)

        time.Sleep(delay) // Wait before retrying

    }

    return errors.New("operation failed after retries")

}


func main() {

    err := retryOperation(fetchData, 3, time.Second)

    if err != nil {

        fmt.Println("Final error:", err)

    }

}
```

■ Why Use Retries?

- Useful for **intermittent failures** (network, database, APIs).
- Prevents **immediate hard failures** in distributed systems.

Using Fallbacks for Resilience

If retries fail, use a **fallback mechanism** (e.g., return cached data).

✔ Example: Fallback Strategy

go

CopyEdit

```go
func fetchDataWithFallback() string {
    err := fetchData()
    if err != nil {
        fmt.Println("Error occurred, using cached data")
        return "Cached Data"
    }
    return "Live Data"
}
```

■ Fallbacks ensure better user experience during failures.

6.6. Logging and Debugging Errors in Production

Logging is essential for **troubleshooting and monitoring** application failures.

Best Practices for Logging Errors

✔ Use Structured Logging

- Instead of plain fmt.Println(), use **structured loggers** like logrus or zap.

✔ **Example: Logging Errors with Context**

go

CopyEdit

```go
package main

import (
    "github.com/sirupsen/logrus"
)

var log = logrus.New()

func main() {
    err := errors.New("database connection failed")
    log.WithFields(logrus.Fields{
        "module": "database",
        "error":  err,
    }).Error("Critical error occurred")
}
```

■ **Why Structured Logging?**

- Logs contain **structured key-value pairs** (e.g., module: database, error: connection failed).
- Makes searching logs **easier** in production.

Monitoring Errors in Production

- **Use Log Aggregation Services:**

  - **Centralize logs** using tools like **ELK Stack (Elasticsearch, Logstash, Kibana)**.
  - Cloud-based logging: **AWS CloudWatch, Google Stackdriver, or Datadog**.

- **Capture and Alert on Errors:**

  - Integrate with **Sentry** or **Prometheus** to **detect and alert on recurring errors**.

✔ **Example: Capturing Errors for Alerts**

go

CopyEdit

```
import "github.com/getsentry/sentry-go"

func main() {
  sentry.Init(sentry.ClientOptions{
    Dsn: "your-sentry-dsn",
  })
  defer sentry.Flush(2 * time.Second)

  sentry.CaptureMessage("Something went wrong!")
}
```

■ **Proactively capturing errors helps prevent major failures.**

110

- **Use custom error types** for structured error handling.
- **Always propagate errors up the stack with context**.
- **Implement retries for transient failures** (e.g., network errors).
- **Use structured logging and monitoring tools in production**.

Chapter 7: Testing, Debugging, and Code Quality

Testing is essential for writing **robust, maintainable, and bug-free** Go applications. Go provides a **built-in testing framework** that simplifies unit, integration, and performance testing. This chapter explores Go's testing tools and best practices for writing **effective unit and integration tests**.

7.1. Go's Built-in Testing Framework

Go has a **built-in testing framework** that allows developers to write and run tests without relying on external libraries. It is located in the testing **package**, and tests are executed using the go test command.

Basic Structure of a Go Test File

- Test files are stored **in the same package** as the code being tested.
- The test file name must end with _test.go.
- Each test function must start with Test and take t *testing.T as an argument.

✔ Example: Writing a Simple Unit Test

```go
package mathutil

import (
    "testing"
)

// Function to test
func Add(a, b int) int {
    return a + b
}

// Unit test for Add function
func TestAdd(t *testing.T) {
```

```go
    result := Add(2, 3)
    expected := 5
    if result != expected {
        t.Errorf("Add(2, 3) = %d; want %d", result, expected)
    }
}
```

💡 **Run the test with:**

sh

go test

⬛ **If the test passes, you see:**

sh

ok   mathutil   0.002s

✖ **If the test fails, Go prints an error message with details.**

Using t.Fatalf(), t.Logf(), and t.Skip() in Tests

Function	Purpose
t.Errorf("message")	Reports a test failure but continues execution.
t.Fatalf("message")	Reports a test failure and **stops execution** immediately.
t.Logf("message")	Logs a message (useful for debugging test cases).
t.Skip("reason")	Skips a test (useful for conditional testing).

✔ **Example: Using t.Fatalf() to Stop Execution on Failure**

go

```go
func TestDivide(t *testing.T) {
    result, err := Divide(10, 0)
    if err == nil {
```

```
      t.Fatalf("Expected error but got none")
   }
   t.Logf("Expected error received: %v", err)
}
```

💡 Use t.Fatalf() when failing the test should stop further execution.

Table-Driven Testing in Go

Table-driven tests allow you to **test multiple inputs efficiently**.

✔ **Example: Table-Driven Testing**

go

```
func TestAddTableDriven(t *testing.T) {
   testCases := []struct {
      a, b    int
      expected int
   }{
      {2, 3, 5},
      {10, 5, 15},
      {-1, -2, -3},
   }

   for _, tc := range testCases {
      result := Add(tc.a, tc.b)
      if result != tc.expected {
         t.Errorf("Add(%d, %d) = %d; want %d", tc.a, tc.b, result, tc.expected)
      }
   }
}
```


■ **Advantages of Table-Driven Testing:**

- Reduces **code duplication**.
- Makes it **easy to add more test cases**.

114

- Improves test readability.

Running Tests with Coverage Analysis

To measure **how much code is covered by tests**, use:

sh

```
go test -cover
```

✔ **Example Output:**

sh

```
PASS
coverage: 85.0% of statements
ok      mathutil        0.003s
```

■ **Why Use Code Coverage?**

- Identifies **untested parts** of the code.
- Helps improve **test completeness**.

7.2. Unit Testing vs. Integration Testing in Go

Understanding the difference between **unit and integration tests** is crucial for **maintaining a healthy codebase**.

What is Unit Testing?

Unit testing ensures that **individual functions** work correctly **in isolation**.

✔ **Characteristics of Unit Tests:**

- Test a **single function or method**.
- Do **not depend on external services** (databases, APIs).

115

- Run **quickly** and help in debugging logic errors.

Example: Unit Testing a Standalone Function

go

```go
func Multiply(a, b int) int {
    return a * b
}

func TestMultiply(t *testing.T) {
    result := Multiply(4, 5)
    expected := 20
    if result != expected {
        t.Errorf("Multiply(4,5) = %d; want %d", result, expected)
    }
}
```

■ Unit tests should be simple, independent, and fast.

What is Integration Testing?

Integration tests verify how **different components interact together**.

✔ **Characteristics of Integration Tests:**

- Test interactions between **multiple components** (e.g., API calls, database queries).
- Often require **mocking or test databases**.
- Run **slower than unit tests** but provide **better real-world validation**.

Example: Integration Testing with a Database

Integration tests often require **setup and teardown**.

✔ Example: Testing a Database Query

go

```go
package repository

import (
    "database/sql"
    "testing"
    _ "github.com/mattn/go-sqlite3"
)

// Sample function to test
func GetUser(db *sql.DB, id int) (string, error) {
    var username string
    err := db.QueryRow("SELECT username FROM users WHERE id=?",
id).Scan(&username)
    return username, err
}

func TestGetUser(t *testing.T) {
    db, err := sql.Open("sqlite3", ":memory:")
    if err != nil {
        t.Fatalf("Failed to open database: %v", err)
    }
    defer db.Close()

    // Create test table
    db.Exec("CREATE TABLE users (id INTEGER PRIMARY KEY, username TEXT)")
    db.Exec("INSERT INTO users (id, username) VALUES (1, 'testuser')")

    username, err := GetUser(db, 1)
    if err != nil || username != "testuser" {
        t.Errorf("GetUser failed: got %s, want testuser", username)
    }
}
```

117

■ **Key Takeaways from Integration Testing:**

- Uses a **real or test database**.
- Ensures **components work together** correctly.
- Requires **setup and teardown** to **reset the test environment**.

Comparing Unit vs. Integration Testing

Feature	Unit Testing	Integration Testing
Scope	Individual function	Multiple components
Dependencies	None (isolated)	Requires external services (DB, API)
Speed	Fast	Slower due to setup
Failure Impact	Low, affects a single function	High, affects system behavior
Use Case	Validating function logic	Ensuring system reliability

■ **Unit tests** are the foundation of a **robust test suite**, while **integration tests** ensure smooth collaboration between components.

- **Go's built-in testing framework** (testing package) makes testing easy.
- **Unit tests** verify individual functions **in isolation**.
- **Integration tests** validate **multiple components working together**.
- **Table-driven testing** simplifies writing multiple test cases.
- **Test coverage analysis** helps identify untested code.

By mastering **unit and integration testing**, Go developers can **write reliable, bug-free, and maintainable code**.

Ensuring that Go applications are **testable, debuggable, and maintainable** requires more than just writing tests. Developers must structure their code for **testability**, apply effective **debugging techniques**, and use **Go's static analysis tools** to enforce best practices.

7.3. Testable Code: Writing Functions and Methods with Testability in Mind

Why Testability Matters

Code that is **hard to test** is often **hard to maintain**. Writing **testable code** ensures that:
✔ Bugs are **caught early** before reaching production.
✔ Code is **modular and loosely coupled**, making it easier to refactor.
✔ Unit tests remain **fast and reliable**.

Best Practices for Writing Testable Code

1 Use Dependency Injection Instead of Hardcoded Dependencies

🔔 Bad Example: Hardcoded Dependencies (Difficult to Test)

go

```go
type Service struct {
    db *sql.DB
}

func (s *Service) FetchData() string {
    row := s.db.QueryRow("SELECT data FROM table")
    var data string
    row.Scan(&data)
    return data
}
```

119

✘ Why is this bad?

- The function depends **directly on a real database**.
- Tests would require **a real database setup**.

✔ Good Example: Using Dependency Injection (Easier to Test)

go

```go
type DataStore interface {

    GetData() string

}


type Service struct {

    store DataStore

}


func (s *Service) FetchData() string {

    return s.store.GetData()

}


// Mock implementation for testing

type MockStore struct{}


func (m MockStore) GetData() string {

    return "mocked data"
```

120

```
}
```

■ Now, the Service can be tested using MockStore instead of a real database.

2 Write Small, Single-Responsibility Functions

- Functions should **do one thing well** to make them **easier to test**.

✔ Example: Testable, Small Functions

go

CopyEdit

```go
func CalculateTax(price float64, rate float64) float64 {

    return price * rate

}
```

♥ Functions that perform only one task are easier to write tests for.

3 Avoid Global State

▲ Bad Example: Using Global Variables

go

```go
var cache = map[string]string{}


func GetCachedValue(key string) string {
```

```go
    return cache[key]
}
```

✖ Why is this bad?

- Tests might **interfere with each other** because they modify global state.

✔ Good Example: Passing Dependencies

go

```go
func GetCachedValue(cache map[string]string, key string) string {
    return cache[key]
}
```

■ **Each test can now provide its own cache, avoiding conflicts.**

7.4. Debugging Techniques for Large Go Projects

Debugging in Go requires **a combination of tools, logging, and structured tracing**.

☐ Using fmt.Println() **for Quick Debugging**

The simplest way to debug is to print variables.

122

✔ Example: Printing Debug Information

go

```go
func divide(a, b float64) float64 {

    fmt.Println("Debug: a =", a, "b =", b)

    return a / b

}
```

🔺 Limitations:

- Clutters the codebase.
- Not useful for large applications.

② Using log for Better Debugging

Go's log package provides **timestamped logs**.

✔ Example: Logging Errors

go

```go
import "log"


func divide(a, b float64) float64 {
    if b == 0 {
        log.Println("Error: Division by zero")
        return 0
```

```
    }

    return a / b

}
```

■ **Better than** fmt.Println(), **but not structured logging.**

3 Using delve for Interactive Debugging

delve (dlv) is Go's interactive debugger.

✔ **Installing delve:**

sh

go install github.com/go-delve/delve/cmd/dlv@latest

✔ **Running a Go program in debug mode:**

sh

dlv debug main.go

💡 **Allows setting breakpoints, stepping through code, and inspecting variables.**

4 Debugging Goroutines

✔ List active goroutines:

sh

```
dlv goroutines
```

✔ Trace execution flow:

sh

```
dlv trace functionName
```

■ **This is useful for debugging concurrency issues.**

7.5. Using Go Tools for Static Analysis

Static analysis tools help **detect bugs, inefficiencies, and security issues** before running the program.

1 go vet - Detect Common Mistakes

✔ Example: Running go vet

sh

```
go vet ./...
```

125

■ Finds suspicious constructs like mismatched format specifiers in fmt.Printf().

2 golangci-lint - Linting and Code Quality

✔ **Installing golangci-lint:**

sh

```
go install github.com/golangci/golangci-lint/cmd/golangci-lint@latest
```

✔ **Running a full linting check:**

sh

```
golangci-lint run
```

■ Detects unused variables, incorrect struct tags, and more.

3 staticcheck - Advanced Static Analysis

✔ **Installing staticcheck:**

sh

```
go install honnef.co/go/tools/cmd/staticcheck@latest
```

✔ **Running static analysis:**

sh

```
staticcheck ./...
```

■ Detects dead code, performance issues, and unnecessary conversions.

7.6. Linting and Code Formatting Best Practices

☐1 Use gofmt for Automatic Code Formatting

✔ **Run gofmt to format Go files:**

sh

```
gofmt -w main.go
```

■ Enforces consistent spacing, indentation, and syntax.

☐2 Use goimports for Organizing Imports

✔ **Install and run goimports:**

sh

```
go install golang.org/x/tools/cmd/goimports@latest
goimports -w .
```

127

■ Automatically sorts and formats imports.

3 Enforce Linting with CI/CD

✔ **Example: Adding** golangci-lint **to GitHub Actions**

yaml

```
name: Go Lint
on: [push, pull_request]
jobs:
  lint:
    runs-on: ubuntu-latest
    steps:
      - uses: actions/checkout@v2
      - uses: golangci/golangci-lint-action@v2
```

■ **Ensures all commits meet linting standards before merging.**

- **Testability** is improved with **dependency injection, small functions, and avoiding global state**.
- **Debugging tools like** delve **and structured logging** help diagnose issues effectively.
- **Static analysis** (go vet, golangci-lint, staticcheck) prevents common coding mistakes.

128

- **Formatting and linting** (gofmt, goimports, golangci-lint) enforce coding standards.

Chapter 8: Go and DevOps: Deployment, CI/CD, and Cloud

Modern software development requires **efficient deployment strategies, automation, and cloud integration**. Go's **small binary size, performance, and ease of cross-compilation** make it an excellent choice for cloud-native applications. This chapter covers **containerizing Go applications with Docker** and **Kubernetes best practices** for deployment and scaling.

8.1. Containerizing Go Applications with Docker

Why Use Docker for Go Applications?

Docker **encapsulates applications** in lightweight, portable containers. This ensures that Go applications **run consistently** across different environments.

✔ **Benefits of Dockerizing Go Applications:**

- Ensures **consistent deployment** across different machines.
- Reduces **dependency conflicts** by packaging everything into a container.
- Improves **scalability** by making it easy to deploy across clusters.

Step 1: Writing a Minimal Go Web Server

Let's create a simple **Go HTTP server** to demonstrate containerization.

✔ **File:** main.go

```go
CopyEdit
package main

import (
    "fmt"
    "net/http"
)
```

```go
func handler(w http.ResponseWriter, r *http.Request) {
    fmt.Fprintf(w, "Hello, Dockerized Go!")
}

func main() {
    http.HandleFunc("/", handler)
    fmt.Println("Starting server on :8080")
    http.ListenAndServe(":8080", nil)
}
```

■ **This is a basic Go web server listening on port 8080.**

Step 2: Writing a Dockerfile for Go

A **Dockerfile** is a script that defines how to **build and run** a Docker container.

✔ **File: Dockerfile**

```dockerfile
dockerfile
CopyEdit
# Use official Golang image to build the binary
FROM golang:1.20 AS builder

# Set working directory
WORKDIR /app

# Copy the source code
COPY . .

# Download dependencies and build the binary
RUN go mod tidy
RUN go build -o app

# Use a lightweight image for the final container
FROM alpine:latest
```

```
# Set working directory in final image
WORKDIR /root/

# Copy the compiled binary from the builder stage
COPY --from=builder /app/app .

# Expose port 8080
EXPOSE 8080

# Command to run the application
CMD ["./app"]
```

■ Why Use a Multi-Stage Build?

- Reduces the final container size by **compiling the Go binary in a separate builder stage**.
- Uses **Alpine Linux** (5 MB) instead of the **Golang base image** (800 MB), reducing overhead.

Step 3: Building and Running the Docker Container

☐1☐ **Build the Docker Image:**

```sh
CopyEdit
docker build -t go-app .
```

☐2☐ **Run the Container:**

```sh
CopyEdit
docker run -p 8080:8080 go-app
```

3 **Test the Application:**

sh
CopyEdit
curl http://localhost:8080

■ **Your Go app is now running in a Docker container.**

Step 4: Optimizing Docker Image Size

For ultra-lightweight images, use scratch as the base image:
✔ **Minimal Dockerfile (Go Static Binary)**

dockerfile
CopyEdit
```
FROM golang:1.20 AS builder
WORKDIR /app
COPY . .
RUN go mod tidy && go build -o app

# Use scratch (empty base image)
FROM scratch
COPY --from=builder /app/app .
CMD ["./app"]
```

■ **Final Image Size:** Only ~5MB, instead of **800MB**.

Step 5: Running Containers in Production

✔ **Running Docker Containers in Detached Mode**

sh
CopyEdit
```
docker run -d -p 8080:8080 go-app
```

✔ **Scaling with Docker Compose** (docker-compose.yml)

yaml
CopyEdit

```yaml
version: '3.7'

services:
  web:
    build: .
    ports:
      - "8080:8080"
    restart: always
```

Run with:

sh
CopyEdit

```sh
docker-compose up -d
```

■ This setup ensures automated restarts and scaling across multiple instances.

8.2. Kubernetes Best Practices for Go Applications

Why Use Kubernetes for Go Applications?

Kubernetes **orchestrates** containers across multiple servers, enabling:
✔ **Automated scaling** based on CPU/memory usage.
✔ **Rolling updates and zero-downtime deployments**.
✔ **Self-healing applications** that restart failed containers.

Step 1: Writing a Kubernetes Deployment for a Go App

✔ **File:** deployment.yaml

yaml
CopyEdit

```yaml
apiVersion: apps/v1
```

```yaml
kind: Deployment
metadata:
 name: go-app
spec:
 replicas: 3
 selector:
  matchLabels:
   app: go-app
 template:
  metadata:
   labels:
    app: go-app
  spec:
   containers:
   - name: go-app
     image: go-app:latest
     ports:
     - containerPort: 8080
     readinessProbe:
      httpGet:
       path: /
       port: 8080
      initialDelaySeconds: 5
      periodSeconds: 10
     livenessProbe:
      httpGet:
       path: /
       port: 8080
      initialDelaySeconds: 5
      periodSeconds: 10
```

■ **Key Features of This Kubernetes Deployment:**
✔ **Three replicas** for high availability.
✔ **Health checks (liveness and readiness probes)** ensure stability.
✔ **Rolling updates with zero downtime**.

Step 2: Exposing the Go Application with a Service

✔ **File:** service.yaml

yaml
CopyEdit

```yaml
apiVersion: v1
kind: Service
metadata:
  name: go-app-service
spec:
  selector:
    app: go-app
  ports:
    - protocol: TCP
      port: 80
      targetPort: 8080
  type: LoadBalancer
```

■ **This makes the Go app accessible via a Kubernetes LoadBalancer.**

Step 3: Deploying the Go Application to Kubernetes

1️⃣ **Apply Deployment and Service Configuration:**

sh
CopyEdit

```sh
kubectl apply -f deployment.yaml
kubectl apply -f service.yaml
```

2️⃣ **Check Running Pods:**

sh
CopyEdit

```sh
kubectl get pods
```

3 **Get the External IP of the Service:**

sh
CopyEdit
kubectl get service go-app-service

◼ **Now, the Go application is running in a Kubernetes cluster.**

Step 4: Scaling Go Applications in Kubernetes

✔ **Manually Scaling Up/Down:**

sh
CopyEdit
kubectl scale deployment go-app --replicas=5

✔ **Autoscaling Based on CPU Usage:**

sh
CopyEdit
kubectl autoscale deployment go-app --cpu-percent=50 --min=2 --max=10

◼ **Kubernetes will automatically adjust the number of instances based on demand.**

Step 5: Rolling Updates for Zero Downtime Deployments

✔ **Update the Deployment with a New Image Version:**

sh
CopyEdit
kubectl set image deployment/go-app go-app=go-app:v2

137

✔ **Check Rolling Update Status:**

sh
CopyEdit
```
kubectl rollout status deployment/go-app
```

✔ **Rollback in Case of Issues:**

sh
CopyEdit
```
kubectl rollout undo deployment/go-app
```

■ **Ensures seamless updates without downtime.**

✔ **Dockerizing Go applications** ensures portability and consistency.
✔ **Using multi-stage builds** reduces image size for efficient deployment.
✔ **Kubernetes best practices** include health checks, autoscaling, and rolling updates.
✔ **Load balancing and service discovery** in Kubernetes improve reliability.

8.3. Automating CI/CD Pipelines with Go

Why Automate CI/CD?

A **Continuous Integration and Continuous Deployment (CI/CD)** pipeline automates:
✔ **Code building and testing** after every commit.
✔ **Containerization and deployment** to production.
✔ **Rollback mechanisms** for failed deployments.

■ **Benefits of CI/CD for Go Applications:**

- **Reduces manual intervention** in deployments.
- **Detects bugs early** through automated testing.
- **Ensures fast, reliable releases** using Git workflows.

Setting Up a GitHub Actions CI/CD Pipeline for Go

Step 1: Create a .github/workflows/go-ci.yml File

✔ GitHub Actions CI/CD Workflow for Go:

yaml
CopyEdit
```yaml
name: Go CI/CD Pipeline

on:
  push:
    branches:
      - main
  pull_request:
    branches:
      - main

jobs:
  build:
    runs-on: ubuntu-latest
    steps:
      - name: Checkout Code
        uses: actions/checkout@v3

      - name: Set up Go
        uses: actions/setup-go@v3
        with:
          go-version: 1.20

      - name: Install Dependencies
        run: go mod tidy

      - name: Run Unit Tests
        run: go test ./...

      - name: Build Application
        run: go build -o app

      - name: Build and Push Docker Image
```

```
    run: |
      echo "${{ secrets.DOCKER_PASSWORD }}" | docker login -u "${{
secrets.DOCKER_USERNAME }}" --password-stdin
        docker build -t myrepo/go-app:latest .
        docker push myrepo/go-app:latest

    - name: Deploy to Kubernetes
      run: kubectl apply -f k8s/deployment.yaml
```

■ How It Works:

- Runs **unit tests** and **builds the Go binary**.
- Creates a **Docker image** and pushes it to Docker Hub.
- Deploys the app to a **Kubernetes cluster**.

Setting Up a GitLab CI/CD Pipeline for Go

✔ **File:** .gitlab-ci.yml

```yaml
yaml
CopyEdit
stages:
  - test
  - build
  - deploy

test:
  stage: test
  script:
    - go test ./...

build:
  stage: build
  script:
    - go build -o app

deploy:
```

```
stage: deploy
script:
  - kubectl apply -f k8s/deployment.yaml
```

◼ **This pipeline ensures automated deployment for Go apps on GitLab.**

8.4. Monitoring and Observability with Prometheus and Grafana

Why Use Prometheus and Grafana?

- **Prometheus** collects real-time metrics from Go applications.
- **Grafana** visualizes Prometheus data with **dashboards and alerts**.

◼ **Key Metrics for Go Applications:**
✔ CPU and memory usage (runtime.ReadMemStats)
✔ Goroutines count (runtime.NumGoroutine())
✔ HTTP request latency (http.HandleFunc())

Step 1: Instrumenting a Go Application with Prometheus

✔ **Install Prometheus Client Library:**

sh
CopyEdit
```
go get github.com/prometheus/client_golang/prometheus
```


✔ **Expose Metrics in a Go HTTP Server:**

go
CopyEdit
```
package main

import (
    "github.com/prometheus/client_golang/prometheus"
    "github.com/prometheus/client_golang/prometheus/promhttp"
    "net/http"
)
```

141

```
// Define a Prometheus metric
var requestCount = prometheus.NewCounter(
  prometheus.CounterOpts{
     Name: "http_requests_total",
     Help: "Total number of HTTP requests",
  })

func handler(w http.ResponseWriter, r *http.Request) {
  requestCount.Inc()
  w.Write([]byte("Hello, Prometheus!"))
}

func main() {
  prometheus.MustRegister(requestCount)
  http.Handle("/metrics", promhttp.Handler()) // Expose metrics
  http.HandleFunc("/", handler)

  http.ListenAndServe(":8080", nil)
}
```

■ **Access Prometheus Metrics at:**

sh
CopyEdit
http://localhost:8080/metrics

Step 2: Running Prometheus and Grafana in Kubernetes

✔ **Deploy Prometheus to Kubernetes:**

yaml
CopyEdit
apiVersion: monitoring.coreos.com/v1
kind: ServiceMonitor
metadata:
  name: go-app-monitor

142

```
spec:
 selector:
  matchLabels:
   app: go-app
 endpoints:
 - port: http
   path: /metrics
```

■ This collects metrics from the Go application and visualizes them in Grafana.

8.5. Scaling Go Services in Cloud Environments

Go applications need **dynamic scaling** in production. Kubernetes and cloud providers provide **horizontal and vertical scaling** strategies.

Horizontal Scaling: Adding More Instances

✔ Example: Autoscaling Go Services in Kubernetes

sh
CopyEdit
```
kubectl autoscale deployment go-app --cpu-percent=50 --min=2 --max=10
```

■ Automatically adjusts the number of replicas based on CPU usage.

Vertical Scaling: Increasing Resource Limits

✔ Example: Configuring Resource Limits in Kubernetes

yaml
CopyEdit
```
resources:
 limits:
  cpu: "1"
  memory: "512Mi"
```

143

```
requests:
  cpu: "250m"
  memory: "128Mi"
```

■ **Allocates CPU and memory resources efficiently.**

8.6. Writing Cloud-Native Applications with Go

Key Principles of Cloud-Native Go Applications

- ◆ **Stateless Services:** Store session data in **Redis** instead of memory.
- ◆ **RESTful and gRPC APIs:** Use **gRPC** for high-performance communication.
- ◆ **12-Factor App Methodology:**
- ✔ Configurations in **environment variables**
- ✔ Logs as **event streams**
- ✔ Dependencies declared in go.mod

Example: Writing a Cloud-Native Go Microservice

✔ **Microservice:** user-service.go

go
CopyEdit
```
package main

import (
    "encoding/json"
    "net/http"
    "os"
)

type User struct {
    ID   int    `json:"id"`
    Name string `json:"name"`
}
```

```go
func getUser(w http.ResponseWriter, r *http.Request) {
    user := User{ID: 1, Name: "John Doe"}
    json.NewEncoder(w).Encode(user)
}

func main() {
    port := os.Getenv("PORT")
    if port == "" {
        port = "8080"
    }

    http.HandleFunc("/user", getUser)
    http.ListenAndServe(":"+port, nil)
}
```

■ **Runs in cloud environments with dynamic port configuration.**

Deploying to AWS Lambda (Serverless Go App)

✔ Step 1: Install AWS Lambda Go SDK

sh
CopyEdit
```
go get github.com/aws/aws-lambda-go/lambda
```

✔ Step 2: Write a Lambda Function

go
CopyEdit
```go
package main

import (
    "context"
    "fmt"
    "github.com/aws/aws-lambda-go/lambda"
```

145

```
)

func handler(ctx context.Context, name string) (string, error) {
    return fmt.Sprintf("Hello, %s!", name), nil
}

func main() {
    lambda.Start(handler)
}
```

■ Deploy the function to AWS Lambda for serverless execution.

✔ **CI/CD pipelines automate deployment** using GitHub Actions or GitLab CI.
✔ **Prometheus and Grafana provide real-time monitoring** for Go applications.
✔ **Kubernetes scaling ensures high availability** with autoscaling strategies.
✔ **Cloud-native design patterns enable scalable, distributed Go services.**

By integrating **automation, observability, and cloud-native best practices**, Go developers can build **scalable, resilient applications** for modern cloud environments.

Chapter 9: Microservices and API Design with Go

Microservices and APIs are at the core of modern software architecture, enabling scalable, modular, and efficient communication between services. Go, with its lightweight concurrency model and built-in HTTP capabilities, is an excellent choice for building **RESTful APIs and gRPC services**. This chapter covers **best practices for designing RESTful APIs in Go and leveraging gRPC for high-performance service-to-service communication**.

9.1. RESTful API Development Best Practices

What is a RESTful API?

A **RESTful API** (Representational State Transfer) is a web service that follows REST principles, providing **stateless communication** between clients and servers using HTTP methods like GET, POST, PUT, and DELETE.

◼ Why Use REST for Microservices?

- Simplicity and ease of implementation.
- Wide adoption across **web and mobile** applications.
- Language-agnostic, allowing **any client** to interact via HTTP.

Best Practices for REST API Development in Go

1 Use the Right HTTP Methods and Status Codes

Each endpoint should use **proper HTTP verbs** and return **meaningful status codes**.

HTTP Method	Purpose	Example Endpoint	Success Code	Failure Code
GET	Retrieve data	/users/{id}	200 OK	404 Not Found
POST	Create new resource	/users	201 Created	400 Bad Request
PUT	Update an existing resource	/users/{id}	200 OK	400 Bad Request
DELETE	Remove a resource	/users/{id}	204 No Content	404 Not Found

✔ **Example: Handling HTTP Methods in Go**

go
CopyEdit
```go
package main

import (
    "encoding/json"
    "net/http"
)

type User struct {
    ID   int    `json:"id"`
    Name string `json:"name"`
}

var users = []User{
    {ID: 1, Name: "John Doe"},
}

// Handle GET requests
func getUser(w http.ResponseWriter, r *http.Request) {
    w.Header().Set("Content-Type", "application/json")
    json.NewEncoder(w).Encode(users)
}

func main() {
```

148

```go
http.HandleFunc("/users", getUser)
http.ListenAndServe(":8080", nil)
}
```

■ **This example returns a JSON list of users over an HTTP GET request.**

2 Use a Framework for Routing and Middleware

Instead of manually handling routes, use frameworks like gorilla/mux **or** chi.

✔ **Example: Routing with chi**

```go
go
CopyEdit
import (
    "github.com/go-chi/chi/v5"
    "net/http"
)

func main() {
    r := chi.NewRouter()
    r.Get("/users/{id}", getUserHandler)
    http.ListenAndServe(":8080", r)
}
```

■ **Using a router makes APIs more maintainable and flexible.**

3 Implement Request Validation

✔ **Example: Validating JSON Input Using go-playground/validator**

```go
go
CopyEdit
import (
    "github.com/go-playground/validator/v10"
```

149

```go
)

type CreateUserRequest struct {
    Name string `json:"name" validate:"required,min=3"`
}

var validate = validator.New()
```

■ **Ensures API inputs are valid before processing the request.**

4 **Handle Errors Gracefully**

✔ **Example: Returning Structured JSON Errors**

go
CopyEdit
```go
type ErrorResponse struct {
    Message string `json:"message"`
}

func writeErrorResponse(w http.ResponseWriter, status int, msg string) {
    w.WriteHeader(status)
    json.NewEncoder(w).Encode(ErrorResponse{Message: msg})
}
```

■ **Provides clear and structured error messages.**

5 **Use Pagination for Large Data Sets**

✔ **Example: Implementing Pagination**

go
CopyEdit
```go
import (
    "strconv"
```

```
)

func getUsers(w http.ResponseWriter, r *http.Request) {
    page, _ := strconv.Atoi(r.URL.Query().Get("page"))
    limit, _ := strconv.Atoi(r.URL.Query().Get("limit"))
    users := fetchUsersFromDB(page, limit)
    json.NewEncoder(w).Encode(users)
}
```

■ **Prevents excessive data loading for API consumers.**

6 Secure Your API with Authentication and Rate Limiting

✔ Example: Using JWT for Authentication

go
CopyEdit
```
import "github.com/dgrijalva/jwt-go"

// Generate a JWT token
func generateToken(userID int) (string, error) {
    token := jwt.NewWithClaims(jwt.SigningMethodHS256, jwt.MapClaims{
        "user_id": userID,
    })
    return token.SignedString([]byte("secret"))
}
```

■ **JWT authentication ensures secure API access.**

✔ Example: Rate Limiting with golang.org/x/time/rate

go
CopyEdit
```
import "golang.org/x/time/rate"

var limiter = rate.NewLimiter(1, 5) // 1 request per second, burst of 5
```

151

```
func rateLimitedHandler(w http.ResponseWriter, r *http.Request) {
  if !limiter.Allow() {
    http.Error(w, "Too many requests", http.StatusTooManyRequests)
    return
  }
  w.Write([]byte("Request allowed"))
}
```

Prevents API abuse by limiting request rates.

9.2. Using gRPC for High-Performance Communication

Why Use gRPC Instead of REST?

gRPC is a **high-performance RPC (Remote Procedure Call) framework** that
provides:
✔ **Binary serialization** (Protocol Buffers) instead of JSON for faster data transmission.
✔ **Built-in support for streaming requests and responses.**
✔ **Automatic code generation** for clients and servers.

Step 1: Defining a gRPC Service with Protocol Buffers

✔ **File:** user.proto

```
proto
CopyEdit
syntax = "proto3";

package userpb;

service UserService {
  rpc GetUser (UserRequest) returns (UserResponse);
}

message UserRequest {
```

```
  int32 id = 1;
}

message UserResponse {
  int32 id = 1;
  string name = 2;
}
```

■ Defines a gRPC service for fetching user data.

Step 2: Generating Go Code from the Proto File

✔ Install protoc and Go plugins:

sh
CopyEdit
```
go install google.golang.org/protobuf/cmd/protoc-gen-go@latest
go install google.golang.org/grpc/cmd/protoc-gen-go-grpc@latest
```

✔ Generate Go Code:

sh
CopyEdit
```
protoc --go_out=. --go-grpc_out=. user.proto
```

■ This generates the Go implementation for the gRPC service.

Step 3: Implementing the gRPC Server in Go

✔ File: server.go

go
CopyEdit
```
package main
```

153

```go
import (
    "context"
    "fmt"
    "net"

    "google.golang.org/grpc"
    pb "path/to/generated/protobuf/files"
)

type server struct {
    pb.UnimplementedUserServiceServer
}

func (s *server) GetUser(ctx context.Context, req *pb.UserRequest) (*pb.UserResponse, error) {
    return &pb.UserResponse{Id: req.Id, Name: "John Doe"}, nil
}

func main() {
    lis, _ := net.Listen("tcp", ":50051")
    grpcServer := grpc.NewServer()
    pb.RegisterUserServiceServer(grpcServer, &server{})
    fmt.Println("gRPC server running on port 50051")
    grpcServer.Serve(lis)
}
```

█ **The server listens on port 50051 and responds to gRPC calls.**

Step 4: Implementing the gRPC Client in Go

✔ **File:** client.go

```go
go
CopyEdit
package main

import (
```

154

```
    "context"
    "fmt"
    "google.golang.org/grpc"
    pb "path/to/generated/protobuf/files"
)

func main() {
    conn, _ := grpc.Dial("localhost:50051", grpc.WithInsecure())
    defer conn.Close()

    client := pb.NewUserServiceClient(conn)
    response, _ := client.GetUser(context.Background(), &pb.UserRequest{Id: 1})
    fmt.Println("User:", response.Name)
}
```

■ **This client calls the gRPC service and retrieves user data.**

9.3. Handling Authentication and Authorization in APIs

Why Authentication and Authorization Matter

✔ **Authentication** verifies **who the user is**.
✔ **Authorization** determines **what the user can do**.

■ **Common Authentication Methods in Go APIs:**

- **JWT (JSON Web Tokens)** for stateless authentication.
- **OAuth 2.0** for third-party authentication (Google, GitHub, etc.).
- **API Keys** for public access APIs.

155

① Implementing JWT-Based Authentication in Go

✔ Step 1: Install the JWT Library

sh

CopyEdit

```
go get github.com/golang-jwt/jwt/v4
```

✔ Step 2: Generate JWT Token in Go

go

CopyEdit

```go
package auth

import (
    "github.com/golang-jwt/jwt/v4"
    "time"
)

var secretKey = []byte("my_secret_key")

func GenerateJWT(userID int) (string, error) {
    token := jwt.NewWithClaims(jwt.SigningMethodHS256, jwt.MapClaims{
        "user_id": userID,
        "exp":     time.Now().Add(time.Hour * 24).Unix(),
```

156

```
    })

    return token.SignedString(secretKey)

}
```

✔ Step 3: Validate JWT Token in Middleware

go

CopyEdit

```go
func JWTMiddleware(next http.Handler) http.Handler {

    return http.HandlerFunc(func(w http.ResponseWriter, r *http.Request) {

        tokenString := r.Header.Get("Authorization")

        if tokenString == "" {

            http.Error(w, "Missing token", http.StatusUnauthorized)

            return

        }


        token, err := jwt.Parse(tokenString, func(token *jwt.Token) (interface{}, error) {

            return secretKey, nil

        })

        if err != nil || !token.Valid {

            http.Error(w, "Invalid token", http.StatusUnauthorized)

            return

        }
```

```go
    next.ServeHTTP(w, r)
  })
}
```

■ Now, all API routes protected by this middleware will require a valid JWT token.

2 Implementing Role-Based Authorization (RBAC)

✔ Example: Checking User Roles in Middleware

go

CopyEdit

```go
func RoleMiddleware(role string) func(http.Handler) http.Handler {
  return func(next http.Handler) http.Handler {
    return http.HandlerFunc(func(w http.ResponseWriter, r *http.Request) {
      userRole := r.Header.Get("Role") // In a real app, fetch from DB or JWT claims
      if userRole != role {
        http.Error(w, "Forbidden", http.StatusForbidden)
        return
      }
      next.ServeHTTP(w, r)
    })
  }
}
```

158

■ Restricts API access based on user roles.

9.4. Rate Limiting and API Performance Optimization

[1] Implementing Rate Limiting in Go

✔ Install the Rate Limiting Package

sh

CopyEdit

```
go get golang.org/x/time/rate
```

✔ Example: Rate Limiting Middleware

go

CopyEdit

```
package middleware

import (
    "net/http"
    "golang.org/x/time/rate"
)

var limiter = rate.NewLimiter(1, 5) // 1 request per second, burst of 5
```

159

```go
func RateLimitMiddleware(next http.Handler) http.Handler {
    return http.HandlerFunc(func(w http.ResponseWriter, r *http.Request) {
        if !limiter.Allow() {
            http.Error(w, "Too many requests", http.StatusTooManyRequests)
            return
        }
        next.ServeHTTP(w, r)
    })
}
```

■ **Protects against DDoS attacks and excessive API usage.**

2 **Caching Responses with Redis**

✔ **Install Redis Client**

sh

CopyEdit

```
go get github.com/go-redis/redis/v8
```

✔ **Example: Caching API Responses**

go

CopyEdit

```
import (
```

```go
    "context"

    "github.com/go-redis/redis/v8"

    "encoding/json"

    "net/http"

    "time"

)


var ctx = context.Background()

var rdb = redis.NewClient(&redis.Options{

    Addr: "localhost:6379",

})


func getCachedResponse(w http.ResponseWriter, r *http.Request) {

    key := "user:1"

    cachedData, err := rdb.Get(ctx, key).Result()


    if err == nil {

        w.Write([]byte(cachedData))

        return

    }


    data := map[string]string{"id": "1", "name": "John Doe"}
```

```go
jsonData, _ := json.Marshal(data)
rdb.Set(ctx, key, jsonData, time.Minute*5)


w.Write(jsonData)
}
```

■ **Reduces database queries and speeds up API responses.**

9.5. Designing Secure APIs in Go

1 Secure API Endpoints Against Attacks

✔ **Use HTTPS:**

sh

CopyEdit

```sh
http.ListenAndServeTLS(":443", "cert.pem", "key.pem", nil)
```


✔ **Prevent SQL Injection:**

go

CopyEdit

```go
db.QueryRow("SELECT * FROM users WHERE id = ?", userID)
```

✔ Validate and Sanitize User Input:

go

CopyEdit

```
import "github.com/go-playground/validator/v10"

var validate = validator.New()
```

2 Protect Against CSRF Attacks

✔ Use CSRF Tokens in Forms

go

CopyEdit

```
import "github.com/gorilla/csrf"

csrfMiddleware := csrf.Protect([]byte("32-byte-long-secret-key"))
```

■ **Prevents cross-site request forgery.**

9.6. Versioning and Maintaining APIs in Production

1 Why API Versioning Matters

- **Avoids breaking changes** when updating APIs.
- **Supports backward compatibility** for old clients.
- **Allows gradual migration to new features.**

②Methods for API Versioning

Versioning Strategy	Example Endpoint	When to Use
URL Versioning	/v1/users	Simple and widely used
Header Versioning	Accept: application/vnd.api+json; version=2	Useful for clients that support custom headers
Query Parameter	/users?version=1	Less common but allows flexibility

✔ **Example: Handling API Versions in Go**

go

CopyEdit

```go
func getUserV1(w http.ResponseWriter, r *http.Request) {
    w.Write([]byte("User API v1"))
}


func getUserV2(w http.ResponseWriter, r *http.Request) {
    w.Write([]byte("User API v2"))
}


func main() {
    http.HandleFunc("/v1/users", getUserV1)
    http.HandleFunc("/v2/users", getUserV2)
    http.ListenAndServe(":8080", nil)
}
```

■ Maintains multiple API versions without breaking existing clients.

3 Deprecating Old API Versions

✔ **Steps to Deprecate an API Version:**

1. **Announce deprecation** in API documentation.
2. **Use HTTP headers to warn clients.**

go

CopyEdit

```
w.Header().Set("Warning", "299 - Deprecated API version")
```

3. **Gradually remove support after migration.**

Chapter 10: The Future of Go and Emerging Best Practices

Go has evolved into one of the most reliable, efficient, and widely adopted languages for modern development. As the language matures, **new features, emerging trends, and innovative use cases** are shaping its future. This chapter explores **upcoming features in Go, evolving best practices, and Go's role in AI and machine learning**.

10.1. What's Next for Go? Upcoming Features and Trends

1 The Evolution of Go: Past, Present, and Future

Since its release in 2009, Go has been **optimized for simplicity, performance, and scalability**. The language is used for **backend services, microservices, cloud applications, networking, DevOps tools, and more**.

As Go evolves, **new features and trends** continue to refine its capabilities. Some key areas of focus include:
✔ **Improved generics support** for better type safety.
✔ **Enhanced memory management and garbage collection** for high-performance applications.
✔ **Better tooling and developer experience** to improve debugging and profiling.

2 Upcoming Features in Go

🚀 1. Improved Generics and Type Parameters
Go introduced **generics in Go 1.18**, significantly improving **code reusability and type safety**. Future versions will continue **refining generics**, making them:
✔ More **efficient** with reduced runtime overhead.
✔ Easier to use for **standard library functions**.

✔ **Example: Generics for Sorting Different Types**

```
go
CopyEdit
func Min[T int | float64](a, b T) T {
```

```
if a < b {
    return a
}
return b
}
```

■ **Future Go versions will optimize generics performance and type inference.**

🚀 **2. Memory Optimization and Enhanced Garbage Collection**
Go's garbage collector (GC) continues to improve, with:
✔ **Lower GC pause times** for high-performance applications.
✔ **More efficient memory allocation** to reduce CPU overhead.

■ **Future versions will further minimize garbage collection impact, improving real-time applications.**

🚀 **3. Better Dependency Management and Tooling**
Future Go releases will enhance **Go Modules**, making it easier to:
✔ Manage **private modules** and vendor dependencies.
✔ Reduce dependency resolution conflicts.

■ **Expect improvements to go mod commands and better go.sum security.**

🚀 **4. Native Support for WASM (WebAssembly)**
Go has experimental **WebAssembly (WASM) support**, allowing **Go applications to run in browsers**.
✔ Enables **frontend and backend Go development**.
✔ Improves **performance of web-based applications**.

■ **Upcoming versions will improve WASM compatibility and reduce binary size.**

🚀 5. Stronger Security Features

Security remains a top priority in Go's future:

✔ **Better cryptographic libraries** for secure API development.
✔ **Enhanced module authentication** to prevent supply chain attacks.

■ **Expect more security-focused enhancements in Go 1.22 and beyond.**

3 Emerging Trends in Go Development

* **Serverless and Cloud-Native Development**

  * **Go is a top choice for serverless platforms** (AWS Lambda, Google Cloud Functions).
  * Future improvements will enhance **cold-start performance and resource efficiency.**

* **Go for Edge Computing and IoT**

  * Go's **small memory footprint** makes it ideal for **edge computing and IoT applications**.
  * Expect **more optimized Go libraries** for low-power devices.

* **Go for Blockchain and Web3 Development**

  * Many blockchain platforms (**Ethereum, Hyperledger, Cosmos**) are built with Go.
  * Future improvements will focus on **high-performance cryptographic operations**.

■ **Go will continue dominating cloud, DevOps, Web3, and serverless architectures.**

10.2. AI, Machine Learning, and Go: Where It Fits In

1 Go's Role in AI and Machine Learning

While Python dominates AI and ML, Go is increasingly used in **high-performance AI applications**, particularly for:
✔ **Data processing and streaming pipelines.**
✔ **Real-time AI inference in cloud applications.**
✔ **Optimized deep learning with GPU acceleration.**

■ Go is ideal for AI workloads requiring speed, concurrency, and cloud scalability.

2 Machine Learning Libraries for Go

🚀 **1. Gorgonia** – Deep Learning in Go

- Supports **neural networks, tensor operations, and GPU acceleration**.
- Enables **efficient computation graphs** for AI modeling.

✔ **Example: Using Gorgonia for AI Models**

```go
CopyEdit
import "gorgonia.org/gorgonia"

g := gorgonia.NewGraph()
x := gorgonia.NewScalar(g, gorgonia.Float32, gorgonia.WithValue(2.0))
y := gorgonia.NewScalar(g, gorgonia.Float32, gorgonia.WithValue(3.0))

z := gorgonia.Must(gorgonia.Add(x, y))
vm := gorgonia.NewTapeMachine(g)
vm.RunAll()
```

■ Gorgonia enables Go-based deep learning applications.

🚀 **2. Gonum** – Scientific Computing and Data Processing

- Optimized for **statistical analysis and numerical computing**.
- Provides **matrix operations and linear algebra for AI models**.

✔ **Example: Using Gonum for Data Processing**

go
CopyEdit

```
import "gonum.org/v1/gonum/mat"

func main() {
    matrix := mat.NewDense(2, 2, []float64{1, 2, 3, 4})
    fmt.Println(matrix)
}
```

⬛ **Gonum is ideal for AI-driven analytics and mathematical computations.**

🚀 **3. GoML** – Machine Learning in Go

- Provides algorithms for **clustering, classification, and regression**.
- Useful for **recommendation engines and fraud detection**.

✔ **Example: GoML Classification Model**

go
CopyEdit

```
import "github.com/sjwhitworth/golearn"

func main() {
    model := golearn.NewDecisionTree()
    model.Fit(data)
    prediction := model.Predict(newData)
}
```

⬛ **GoML simplifies AI model training and prediction in Go.**

3 Real-World Use Cases of AI with Go

✔ **1. Real-Time AI Inference for Cloud Services**

- Go is used for **deploying AI models as microservices.**
- Applications include **chatbots, recommendation engines, and fraud detection.**

✔ **2. High-Performance AI APIs**

- AI companies use Go to **expose deep learning models via APIs.**
- Example: **TensorFlow Serving with Go clients for fast AI predictions.**

✔ **3. AI-Driven Data Streaming with Kafka and Go**

- Go is used for **real-time analytics and fraud detection.**
- AI models in **Kafka streams process large-scale data efficiently.**

■ **Go is emerging as a powerful tool for AI-based cloud microservices.**

What's Next for Go?
✔ Improved **generics, memory management, and garbage collection.**
✔ Stronger **security, WASM support, and dependency management.**
✔ Growth in **serverless, IoT, blockchain, and DevOps applications.**

Go's Role in AI & ML
✔ **Gorgonia, Gonum, and GoML** provide AI capabilities.
✔ **Go powers real-time AI inference and cloud-based ML models.**
✔ **AI-driven microservices and streaming analytics** are emerging trends.

Go's future is **bright, scalable, and cloud-native.** The language continues to evolve with **performance enhancements, security improvements, and AI integrations.**

10.3. Go in Blockchain and High-Performance Computing

1 Why Go is a Top Choice for Blockchain Development

Blockchain applications require:
✔ **Efficiency** – Go's compiled binaries execute faster than interpreted languages like

171

Python.

✔ **Concurrency** – Go's **goroutines** handle thousands of blockchain transactions in parallel.

✔ **Cross-Platform Support** – Compiles **statically linked binaries** for any OS.

■ **Blockchain projects like Ethereum, Hyperledger Fabric, and Cosmos are written in Go** because of these strengths.

2 Go-Based Blockchain Projects

🚀 1. Ethereum (Geth)

- The **Go Ethereum (Geth) client** powers the Ethereum blockchain.
- Geth enables developers to **run Ethereum nodes, deploy smart contracts, and interact with the blockchain.**

✔ **Example: Running an Ethereum Node with Geth**

sh

CopyEdit

```
geth --syncmode "fast" --http --http.addr "localhost" --http.port 8545
```

■ **Geth is optimized for fast blockchain synchronization using Go's concurrency features.**

🚀 2. Hyperledger Fabric

- An enterprise blockchain platform written in Go.
- Used for **private, permissioned blockchain networks**.
- Supports **modular smart contracts and identity management**.

✔ Example: Writing a Smart Contract in Go for Hyperledger Fabric

go

CopyEdit

```
package main

import (
    "github.com/hyperledger/fabric-contract-api-go/contractapi"
)

type SmartContract struct {
    contractapi.Contract
}

func (s *SmartContract) InitLedger(ctx contractapi.TransactionContextInterface) error {
    return ctx.GetStub().PutState("key", []byte("Hello, Blockchain!"))
}
```

■ **Hyperledger Fabric enables secure and scalable enterprise blockchain solutions.**

🚀 **3. Cosmos SDK**

- Cosmos SDK, built in Go, powers **interoperable blockchain networks**.
- Enables developers to **build custom blockchains with Go's efficiency**.

173

✔ Example: Creating a Custom Blockchain Module with Cosmos SDK

go

CopyEdit

```
package mymodule

import (
    "github.com/cosmos/cosmos-sdk/types"
)

func MyHandler(ctx types.Context, msg types.Msg) (*types.Result, error) {
    return &types.Result{}, nil
}
```

■ Cosmos allows blockchain networks to communicate using the Inter-Blockchain Communication (IBC) protocol.

3 High-Performance Computing (HPC) with Go

Go is gaining traction in **HPC applications**, where performance and scalability are key.

■ **Why Use Go for High-Performance Computing?**
✔ **Concurrency for parallel processing** using **goroutines**.
✔ **Lightweight memory usage** compared to Java or C++.
✔ **Fast execution** with a **compiled language**.

174

4 Parallel Computing with Goroutines

✔ Example: Using Goroutines for Parallel Processing

go

CopyEdit

```go
package main

import (
    "fmt"
    "sync"
)

func worker(id int, wg *sync.WaitGroup) {
    defer wg.Done()
    fmt.Printf("Worker %d processing...\n", id)
}

func main() {
    var wg sync.WaitGroup
    for i := 0; i < 10; i++ {
        wg.Add(1)
        go worker(i, &wg)
    }
```

```
wg.Wait()

}
```

■ **This allows Go to execute parallel computations efficiently.**

5 Scientific Computing with Gonum

The **Gonum** package enables numerical and matrix operations in Go.

✔ **Example: Matrix Multiplication in Go**

go

CopyEdit

```
package main

import (
    "fmt"
    "gonum.org/v1/gonum/mat"
)

func main() {
    a := mat.NewDense(2, 2, []float64{1, 2, 3, 4})
    b := mat.NewDense(2, 2, []float64{5, 6, 7, 8})
    var result mat.Dense
    result.Mul(a, b)
```

```
fmt.Println("Result:\n", mat.Formatted(&result))
}
```

■ **Go is a strong alternative to Python for numerical computing and data science applications.**

10.4. When to Choose Go Over Other Languages

Go is often compared to languages like **Python, Rust, Java, and C++**. The best choice depends on **performance, maintainability, and scalability**.

1️⃣ **When to Use Go**

Use Case	Why Choose Go?
Cloud-Native Applications	Optimized for Kubernetes, microservices, and DevOps tools.
High-Performance APIs	Faster than Python and easier to maintain than Java.
Blockchain Development	Ethereum, Hyperledger, and Cosmos SDK are built with Go.
Networking and Distributed Systems	Built-in concurrency with goroutines.
High-Performance Computing (HPC)	Fast execution and low memory usage.

■ **Go is best when performance, scalability, and ease of use are critical.**

2 Go vs. Other Languages

Comparison	Go	Python	Rust	Java
Performance	High	Low	Very High	Medium
Concurrency	Excellent (Goroutines)	Weak (Threading)	Complex	Good (Threads)
Ease of Use	Simple	Easy	Complex	Verbose
Compilation	Fast	Interpreted	Slow	Slow
Best For	APIs, microservices, DevOps. blockchain	Data science. AI, scripting	Systems programming, embedded	Enterprise, large-scale apps

■ Go is simpler than Rust, faster than Python, and more scalable than Java.

10.5. Final Thoughts and Recommendations

1 The Future of Go

- **Go will continue to dominate cloud-native development, APIs, and microservices.**
- **Generics, WASM, and security enhancements** will further expand Go's capabilities.
- **AI and blockchain adoption** in Go will increase as more libraries emerge.

2 Key Takeaways

🚀 **Go is the best choice for:**
✔ **Cloud applications** (Kubernetes, Docker, Terraform).
✔ **API development** (REST, gRPC, GraphQL).
✔ **Blockchain platforms** (Ethereum, Hyperledger, Cosmos SDK).
✔ **High-performance computing and networking.**

🚀 **Go is evolving with:**
✔ **Better generics and performance optimizations.**
✔ **Expanded AI and machine learning capabilities.**
✔ **More adoption in Web3 and cloud environments.**

■ If you're looking for a fast, scalable, and easy-to-learn language, Go is the best choice.

Final Recommendations

1. **Learn Go's concurrency model** – It's a key advantage over Python and Java.
2. **Adopt Go for microservices** – It simplifies API development and scaling.
3. **Use Go for blockchain and Web3** – It's the preferred language for new decentralized platforms.
4. **Stay updated on Go's roadmap** – Generics, security, and cloud-native optimizations are improving fast.

Closing Thoughts

Go has solidified its place in modern **backend development, DevOps, microservices, and cloud computing**. As the language evolves, its **simplicity, efficiency, and scalability** will drive even greater adoption across industries.

🚀 The future of Go is bright, and developers who master it will be well-positioned for success in cloud computing, AI, and blockchain development.

www.ingramcontent.com/pod-product-compliance
Lightning Source LLC
La Vergne TN
LVHW051333050326
832903LV00031B/3515